RANCHO LOS CERRITOS

RANCHO LOS CERRITOS

• PEOPLE WHO SHAPED THE LAND •

DR. LESLIE REESE

Published by The History Press
An imprint of Arcadia Publishing
Charleston, SC
www.historypress.com

Front cover: House. *Rancho Los Cerritos Collection.*

First published 2025

Manufactured in the United States

ISBN 9781467170987
Hardcover ISBN 9781540299758

Library of Congress Control Number: 2025944913

Rancho Los Cerritos circa 2024. *Rancho Los Cerritos Collection.*

CONTENTS

ACKNOWLEDGEMENTS

The idea for a book focusing on the stories of the many people who played a role in the history of the Rancho Los Cerritos over time came out of discussions among members of the Rancho Los Cerritos Volunteer Accessibility Committee, a committee made up of volunteers and staff members dedicated to engaging in work to make the site and its interpretation more accessible, inclusive and engaging for all visitors. Members supported writing of the manuscript from start to finish with enthusiasm, providing constructive review and ideas for initial drafts of each chapter. Many thanks to committee members Alfred Alonso, C.J. British, Alison Bruesehoff, Magda Cervantes, Marcia Harris, Tom Heaton, Andreyina Juarez, Alana Reese, Ron Reese and Laura Wilbanks. RLC executive director Alison Bruesehoff served as book project manager, making the publication a reality. Living history docents Greg Robson and Nancy Voils generously shared materials from their own research on Bixby family history. A special commendation is extended to Magda Cervantes for her work in obtaining permissions for the photographs and images in the book and preparing them for publication. The time and efforts of the reviewers of the manuscript, who provided thoughtful questions, suggestions and critique, are much appreciated.

Writing this book would have been infinitely more difficult without the support of my family. Heartfelt thanks to my husband, Ron, for his unfailing support and understanding; to my daughter, Alana, for her thoughtful feedback and suggestions; and to my niece Kelli Conley, who helped with interview analysis, source selection and manuscript editing and served as a sounding board for ideas. Additional family members Nani, Cricket and Lilo provided faithful accompaniment throughout the writing process.

INTRODUCTION

The significance of Rancho Los Cerritos Historic Site is evidenced in its official designation as a local, state and national historic landmark. As we begin the story of Rancho Los Cerritos, we might well ask: What do we mean by the history of this rancho? Are we referring to the adobe home built in 1844 and its present-day five-acre site? Or do we mean the lands encompassed in the original Spanish land grant, on which several Southern California cities are located today? Does Rancho history begin with the Indigenous people on whose ancestral homeland the Rancho was built? Should we focus on the owners of the Rancho over time—the Nieto, Cota, Temple and Bixby families—or should our scope include all those who lived and worked on Rancho lands? To these questions, this book answers: "All the above!" As Bixby family historian Stephen Dudley put it, "All of these things fit in the picture, and there is no one thread to 'here is *the* story.' There are multiple chapters in different places at different times."

No history can claim to be complete. Limitations of space require selection of facts to include and of experiences to recount. The goal of this book is to bring to the forefront the many people who contributed to the history of the site over time and to connect their experiences with broader trends in California and the nation. These include Tongva shamans and *vaqueros*, Californio settlers and soldiers, ranch owners and sheepherders, cooks, servants, tenant farmers and boardinghouse residents. In understanding their experiences, we can better understand Southern California communities of the present and our own place in them. The book is part of the living legacy of this historic site as a place where the past meets the present and helps shape the future.

CHAPTER 1

"WE ARE ON TONGVA LAND"

The story of Rancho Los Cerritos begins with the land and with the early inhabitants of the land. The Rancho is located on the ancestral and current homelands of the Tongva (Gabrielino) people, who are the past, present and future caretakers of the Los Angeles Basin and Southern Channel Islands. Graton Rancheria leader and educator Greg Sarris writes that for his people "the landscape was nothing less than a richly layered text, a sacred book: each ocean cove, even the smallest seemingly unassuming rock or tract of open grassland—each feature of the natural world was a mnemonic peg on which individuals could see a story connected to other stories and thus know and find themselves home."[1] Tongva elder Craig Torres adds, "Plants are not just 'cultural resources.' Plants are our relatives. They're to be treated with reciprocal respect."[2]

European observers saw the abundance of the land in terms of its potential for settlement. Writings of the first Europeans to arrive in California describe willow-lined rivers, lush wetlands and canyons lined with oak, alder and willow trees. Fray Juan Crespi's diaries of expeditions in 1770 document "large, plentiful, and abundant" stands of oak trees as well as wild strawberries and roses.[3] Scotsman Hugo Reid later described the setting of Mission San Gabriel as a "complete forest of oaks" with a thicket of "wild rose and wild grapevines."[4] It has been said that the diversity and abundance of the flora and fauna of preconquest California would be unrecognizable to twenty-first century Californians.[5]

FIRST PEOPLES: INDIGENOUS POPULATIONS AND CULTURES

The moderate climate and verdant landscape of California, coupled with the Indigenous peoples' management of resources, supported a preconquest population of about 310,000.[6] California was perhaps the most densely populated region north of Mexico at this time and was one of the most linguistically diverse places on earth.[7] California Indians spoke over one hundred different languages, representing roughly one-quarter of all the Indigenous languages of the United States.[8]

The ecological diversity of California was matched by the cultural diversity among the Indigenous groups. From the Yurok in the redwood forests in the north to the Miwok in the acorn-rich foothills of the Sierra Nevada, the Ohlone in the San Francisco Bay area and the Chumash on the southern coast, a multiplicity of different cultures characterized the region. Common across these cultures, however, was gathering of acorns as a basic food staple, weaving of baskets and political organization by villages. A rich oral tradition of storytelling and song to communicate creation stories, impart values and ethics and foster identity characterized the California Indigenous cultures as well. Also common across groups was, and continues to be, a fundamental land use ethic: that one must interact respectfully with nature and coexist with all life forms.[9]

Indigenous people have been documented in the archaeological record occupying the Los Angeles Basin and surrounding areas as early as 8000 BCE.[10] At Rancho Los Cerritos, eleven cogged stones—flat stone discs with notched edges dating from approximately 6750 BCE—were unearthed by a laborer excavating a ditch during the 1930 remodel of the adobe house.[11] Most likely of ritual significance, the cogged stones provide evidence of ancient and long-term occupation of the site. The Tongva people, called Gabrieleño (Gabrielino) by the Spanish settlers based on the incorporation of many of their people into Mission San Gabriel in the eighteenth century, occupied lands that encompassed over 1,500 square miles. Tongva territory extends from the Pacific Ocean to the San Gabriel and the San Bernardino Mountains and includes the southern Channel Islands. The Los Angeles and Santa Ana Rivers run through the heart of the vast watershed region. It is not known whether, prior to conquest, the Tongva had a general name for themselves; at the local level they referred to themselves with reference to their home community.[12] Today four different organizations represent the Tongva people: Gabrielino-Tongva

Cogged stones uncovered during Rancho Los Cerritos remodeling project, 1930. *Rancho Los Cerritos Collection.*

Indian Tribe, Gabrielino/Tongva Nation, Kizh Nation (Gabrieleño Band of Mission Indians) and Gabrieleño San Gabriel Band of Mission Indians (led by the Gabrieleño Tongva Tribal Council).[13]

The land of the Tongva, Tovaangar, was occupied by fifty to one hundred independent yet interconnected villages supporting about five thousand people.[14] The sacred site of Povuu'nga, presently located in east Long Beach on the seventeen acres ceded to California State University, Long Beach, was the "place of emergence," where the Tongva believed their world and their lives began. One of the largest villages was Yaang'na, near the current location of Union Station in downtown Los Angeles. Near the present-day Rancho Los Cerritos adobe home was the village of Tevaaxa'anga.

Tongva villages, which were typically located close to a water source, consisted of clusters of dome-shaped homes, called *kish* or *kiitcha*, which were built using willow branches for the frame and tule (bulrush) layered on the outside. The steep pitch of the roof helped keep out the rain, and the thatch walls allowed air to circulate and remain fresh.[15] In the center of each community was the *yovaar*, or place of worship. The yovaar consisted of a round or oval courtyard surrounded by a brushwork fence and divided into two parts. In one of the parts and sheltered within a fence made of stakes stood a figure representing Chengiichngech, the creator-god of the Gabrielino people.[16] A *temescal*, or sweathouse, was an important part of the village. This semicircular, semisubterranean structure served not only for daily bathing but also for ritual purification.[17]

Tongva villages were independent economic and political entities, and although loosely bound together by language and culture, they were not joined together under a single chief.[18] Each of the villages was governed by a hereditary chief, or *tomyaar*, who was advised by a council of elders. Also pivotal to the life of the community were the shamans, or healers, who could be women among the Gabrielinos. Shamans cured illnesses by sucking the disease from the patient's body using of a steatite (soapstone) pipe.[19] Shamans also named children, predicted the future and possessed the power to control external events.[20] They were responsible for preserving sacred and historical knowledge, memorized and passed by word of mouth to each generation.[21] In his book *The First Angelinos: The Gabrielino Indians of Los Angeles*, scholar William McCawley notes, however, that much of the oral literature was too sacred to be revealed to the uninitiated, and little has survived.[22]

Ritual was a fundamental part of Tongva life, a way of celebrating personal events such as the birth of a child and the onset of puberty as well as reinforcing community ties and values. The Tongva practiced a mourning ceremony, celebrated in memory of those who had passed away in the period since the last ceremony. The eight-day ceremony involved elaborately costumed dancers and singers and the use of

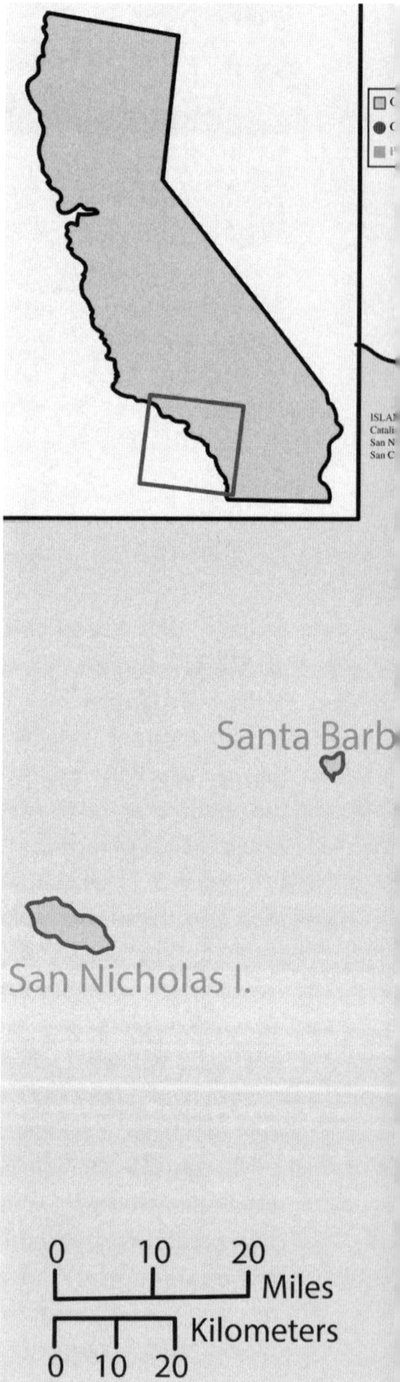

Map of Tongva villages. *Gabrieleno Tongva San Gabriel Band of Mission Indians; used with permission.*

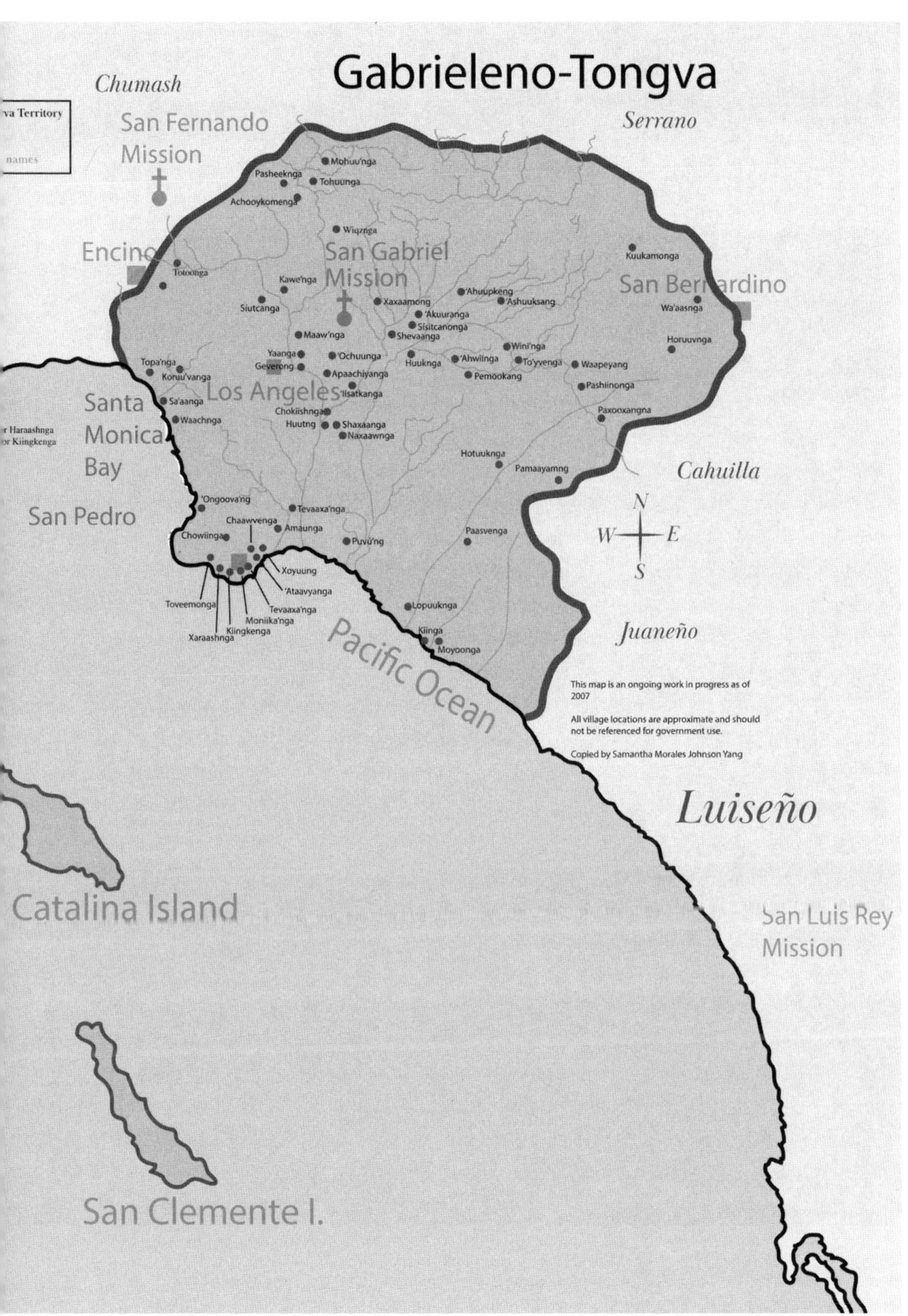
Gabrieleno-Tongva
Chumash
Serrano
Cahuilla
Juaneño
Luiseño
San Fernando Mission
San Gabriel Mission
San Bernardino
Encino
Los Angeles
Santa Monica Bay
San Pedro
Pacific Ocean
Catalina Island
San Clemente I.
San Luis Rey Mission
Mohuu'nga
Pasheeknga
Tohuunga
Achooykomenga
Wiqznga
Totoonga
Kawe'nga
Siutcanga
Xaxaamong
'Ahuupkeng
'Ashuuksang
'Akuuranga
Sísitcanonga
Shevaanga
Maaw'nga
Yaanga
Geverong
'Ochuunga
Apaachiyanga
'Iisatkanga
Huuknga
'Ahwiinga
Wini'nga
To'yvenga
Pemookang
Waapeyang
Pashiinonga
Kuukamonga
Wa'aasnga
Horuuvnga
Paxooxangna
Topa'nga
Koruu'vanga
Sa'aanga
Waachnga
Chokiishnga
Huutng
Shaxaanga
Naxaawnga
Hotuuknga
Pamaayamng
'Ongoova'ng
Tevaaxa'nga
Chaawvenga
Amaunga
Chowiinga
Puvú'ng
Paasvenga
Xoyuung
'Ataavyanga
Toveemonga
Tevaaxa'nga
Moniika'nga
Kiingkenga
Xaraashnga
Lopuuknga
Kiinga
Moyoonga
N
W
E
S
This map is an ongoing work in progress as of 2007
All village locations are approximate and should not be referenced for government use.
Copied by Samantha Morales Johnson Yang

Drawing of a Tongva village. *Friends of the Ballona Wetlands; used with permission.*

images representing the dead. After a person's death, their belongings were cremated along with the body.[23]

Although the Indigenous peoples of California were not warrior societies, warfare between groups was not uncommon, with revenge as the usual motive. Pablo Tac, a Luiseño Indian youth who was sent to study in Rome, wrote one of the few accounts of California mission Indian life by an Indigenous author. Of life prior to the arrival of the Spanish, he stated, "Always there was war, always strife day and night with those who spoke in another language."[24]

Traditional Ecological Knowledge

Although the Indigenous peoples of California are referred to as hunter-gatherers, use of this term tends to obscure the active role that Indigenous people played in the shaping of their environment to maximize and sustain food production. The term *hunter-gatherers* seems to imply that the people did little more than pick, collect or hunt what was readily available in their environment. The term also suggests a binary relation between groups who gather food and those who engage in agriculture. Rather, there is most likely a continuum of practices ranging from foraging to sedentary planting and harvesting of crops.

Tending the wild is a phrase used to describe the many practices utilized by Indigenous peoples of California, including horticultural practices such as pruning, coppicing, sowing, weeding, burning and thinning, to encourage desired plant characteristics and maximize crop yields.[25] Selective burning not only enhanced food crops but also provided better habitats for game. The natural landscapes described by nineteenth-century naturalist John Muir as pristine wilderness were in fact Indigenous gathering areas whose flora had been enhanced and protected over the centuries by selective burning, harvesting and seed scattering.[26]

Acorns, harvested in the fall, formed the staple of the Tongva diet. Acorns were gathered by placing them in a net bag or cone-shaped basket carried with a strap over the forehead.[27] Temporary camps would be set up in the hills to collect acorns from the California black oak, which grew at slightly higher elevations than the coast live oak.[28] Indigenous people also burned the leaves and duff that accumulated under the oak trees in order to kill the insects that would otherwise live there and cause damage to the trees.[29]

To prepare acorns for consumption, the outside shell and acorn cap were discarded, and the meat was removed with an antler or bone tool. The acorn meat was dried and then ground into a rough flour using a mortar. The acorn flour needed to be leached to remove tannins by pouring cold and then hot water over it repeatedly.[30] The Tongva used baskets for the leaching process, unlike some of the other California groups that used a sand filter process.[31]

Tongva women used a *mano*, or handstone, and a *metate*, a portable stone slab, to grind acorns, seeds and other items in food preparation. A soaproot brush was used to clean the metate. The ground acorn meal could then be used to make *atole*, or porridge, and flat cakes. Seeds harvested included chia (sage seeds), which were roasted, and wild oats. Blackberries grew in the wet areas around riverbeds, and Tongva harvested elderberries, currants and prickly pear, among many other food sources.

Food was stored and prepared using a variety of baskets, for which the Tongva were renowned. The different materials used for coiled and twined baskets included tule, rush, deergrass, cattail and willow.[32] Baskets were used for fishing, seed beating and leaching acorn meal as well as for hats, plates and trays. Tongva basketry skills were so highly developed that intricate and tightly woven baskets could be used for carrying water. For longer-term water storage, baskets could be lined with asphaltum (tar) that seeped up from underground deposits. Some of the plants utilized by the Tongva for food, basket-making, medicinal purposes and musical instruments can currently be seen in the Rancho's native garden.[33]

Tongva basket. *Courtesy of Smithsonian Institute National Museum of the American Indian.*

To supplement their plant-based diet, Tongva hunted for game and birds using a variety of methods: bows and arrows, javelins, snares, clubs and throwing sticks. Arrowheads were made from chert or obsidian, flaked to form points, and shafts were made from hardwood or carrizo cane. Hunters sought rabbits, squirrels, deer and antelope. The Tongva fished in rivers and streams as well as in the ocean, using a variety of tools, including spears, hooks, nets and baskets. Hooks were usually fashioned from shell, often abalone, or bone. Conical baskets were used in streams: the fish were driven downstream into the trap. Large nets made of knotted fibers, typically from seagrass, were thrown out from canoes to ensnare fish.[34] Although both men and women worked on the fabrication and repair of the nets, fishing itself was a male activity, as was hunting. For fishing in lagoons, bays and close to shore, the Tongva created canoes made of bundled tule (bulrush). These lightweight canoes could easily be carried.[35]

In order to fish in the open sea, the Tongva constructed a *ti'at* (plank canoe), typically made of redwood from Northern California forests that had washed ashore after storms and of local pine.[36] The Tongva and the Chumash to the north were the only California tribes to construct plank canoes. The inside of the ti'at was coated with a mixture of tar and pine pitch to make the vessel waterproof. Abalone shells were used for the decorative inlays. Ti'ats ranged in length from ten to thirty feet. Shark, halibut, bonito and yellow tail were among the fish caught by Tongva fishermen working collectively in the ti'at using ironwood fishing spears.

The ti'at also facilitated trade along the coast and among the Channel Islands. The mainland Tongva traded acorns, pine nuts, and deer and rabbit skins with islanders for soapstone, beads and skins of sea otters and seals. Easily carved soapstone was used for making bowls as well as effigies in the shape of animals and birds. Effigies served as personal talismans and were thought to impart spiritual power to the owner.[37]

Soapstone items were traded with other groups, such as the Chumash to the north as well as with other Tongva villages. The unit of exchange for trade was a length of shell beads, the standard unit being a string of beads wrapped once around the hand.[38] Through trade with groups as distant as the Mojave near the Colorado River, a greater diversity in food and other resources became possible.

Tending the wild included the cultivation of plants for spiritual purposes as well as for food. Along with other groups in the south, the Tongva practiced

Members of the Ti'at Society paddle their traditional Tongva plank canoe off the coast of Santa Catalina Island. *Courtesy of Frank Magallanes and Althea Edwards.*

the *toalache* (jimson weed) ritual, which included supernatural visions or hallucinations.[39] The toalache drug was ingested by adolescent boys as part of their initiation ritual into adulthood.

The lifeways of the Tongva and other Indigenous people of California were changed irrevocably with the conquest of the region by Spain. The rich watershed land of the Los Angeles Basin was identified as ideal for settlement, and the Tongva were among the first people to experience the impact of Spanish incursion into their homeland.

Initial Contact

The history of Rancho Los Cerritos cannot be fully understood without recognition of the fact that the Rancho was created on Tongva land, seized from the Native people through military force and numerous methods of colonial coercion, including in the realm of religion. The Spanish colony of La Nueva España, established in 1521, included at its height the present country of Mexico as well as Central America and parts of the West Indies, the southwestern and central United States, Florida and the Philippines. The present state of California formed the territory of Alta (or Upper) California, to distinguish it from the peninsula of Baja (or Lower) California to the south. Alta California, on the outermost frontier of the colony of New Spain, was explored by Juan Rodríguez Cabrillo on the galleon *San Salvador* as early as 1542 and was claimed for the Spanish crown.

Later, Sebastián Vizcaíno led an expedition tasked with locating safe harbors in Alta California to be used by Spanish galleons in a triangular trade route. Galleons sailed across the Pacific Ocean from Acapulco to Manila and then, laden with goods from the Orient on their return trip, followed the trade winds to the coast of California around Monterey. This made Monterey a strategic site for a port.

In 1602, Vizcaíno entered and named San Diego Bay. Continuing up the coast, he encountered Tongva people on Catalina Island. From there, he went on to name and describe Monterey Bay. There was little interest in Spanish settlement of the region, however, until the late 1700s. At that time, settlement of the territory began in earnest to fend off possible encroachment by Russia and England.

With the "Sacred Expedition" led by Gaspar de Portolá in 1769 and the establishment of a mission and presidio (fort) at San Diego, Spanish

Statue of Don Gaspar de Portolá. *Courtesy of Barry Swackhamer and the Historical Marker Database.*

settlement of Alta California began. Participation in the Sacred Expedition became a source of pride for later Californio families such as the Nietos and Cotas, future owners of Rancho Los Cerritos. In much the same way that families on the East Coast of the United States proudly cite ancestors who arrived on the *Mayflower*, so too elite Californios proclaimed their longtime roots in Alta California through ancestors who had marched with Portolá.

Captain Gaspar de Portolá, a Catalan military officer and colonial administrator from northeastern Spain, was appointed governor of the province of Las Californias (i.e., Alta and Baja California). He was directed to lead an exploration expedition of Alta California together with Father Junípero Serra, leader of the Franciscan missionaries. Their joint leadership underscored the collaboration of church and crown in the process of colonization.

The expedition included three ships leaving from the port of La Paz in Baja California as well as an overland contingent led by Portolá himself. Portolá's contingent arrived first at San Diego Bay. The ships arrived later,

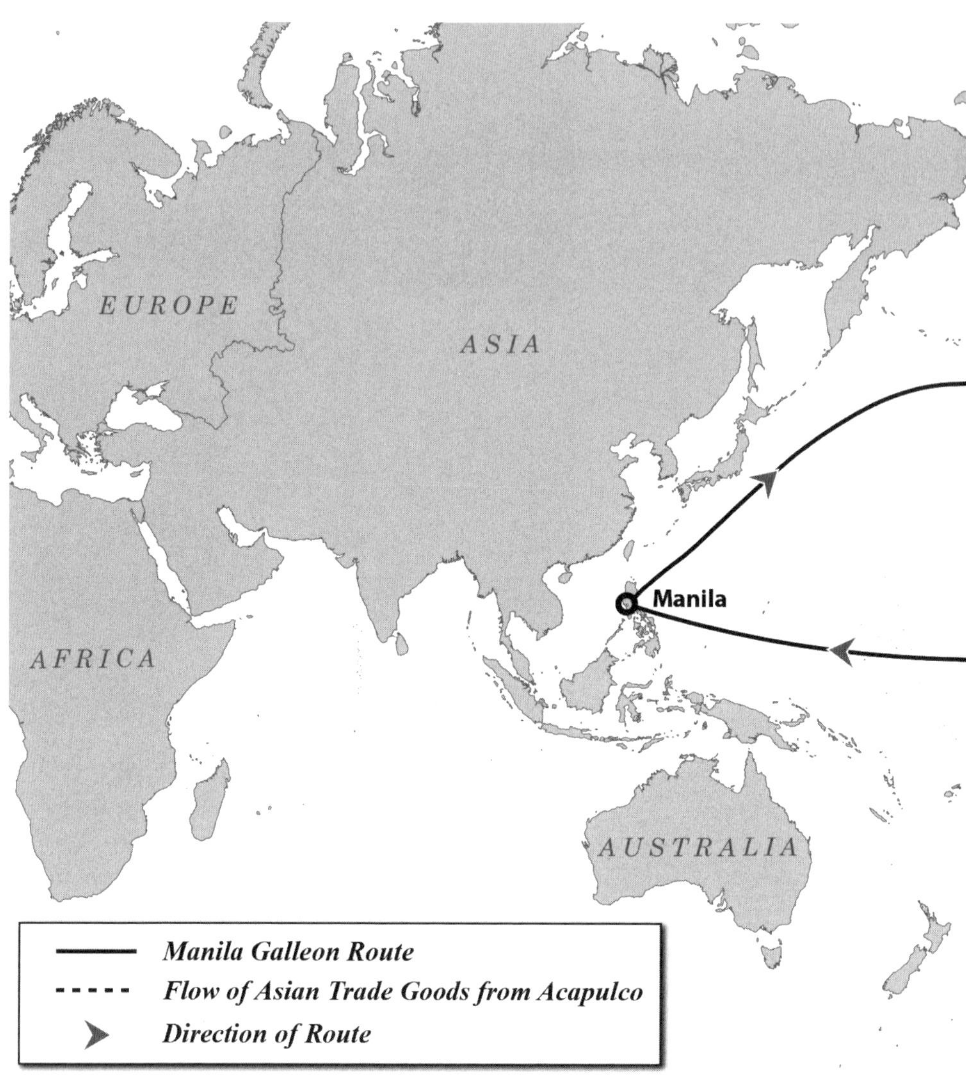

with many of the sailors suffering from scurvy. Portolá left behind fewer than a dozen healthy soldiers to protect Serra's fledgling Mission San Diego de Alcalá and the invalid sailors recuperating there.[40] Portolá continued north, accompanied by Father Crespí, Captain Rivera y Moncada (who would later lead the expedition of settlement of the pueblo of Los Angeles) and Lieutenant Pedro Fages and six of his Catalonian volunteers. The expedition included soldiers, *arrieros* (muleteers) and one hundred mules loaded down with provisions. The aim of the expedition was to establish an overland

Map showing the triangular trade route of the Manila galleons between Acapulco and Manila via the California coast. *Courtesy of the* Oregon Historical Quarterly. *Originally published in "Views Across the Pacific: The Galleon Trade and Its Traces in Oregon,"* Oregon Historical Quarterly *119, no. 2 (Summer 2018). Map by Jesse Nett.*

route to Monterey Bay. They covered two to four leagues (five to ten miles) a day, halting on Sundays long enough to hear mass.

Father Crespí kept journals in which he documented the journey, including descriptions of their encounters with Native peoples. Among these were numerous encounters with the Tongva in the Los Angeles Basin where Rancho Los Cerritos would later be located.

> En este Arroyo nos salieron otros tantos Gentiles de este Paraje, tamvién armados, como a saludarnos, se quedaron todos: es toda gente mui manza y docil [original spelling]. *In this arroyo several more Gentiles from this spot came towards us, also armed, as if to greet us, and all stayed there: they are all very meek and docile people.*[41]

Luiseño Indian Pablo Tac gave a more nuanced description of the arrival of a missionary to his people's land.[42]

> *The captain* [said] *perhaps in his language "Hichsom iva haluon, puluchajam cham quinai." "What is it you seek here? Get out of our country!" But they did not understand him, and they answered him in Spanish, and the captain began with signs, and the Fernandino, understanding him, gave him gifts and in this manner made him his friend. The captain, turning to his people (as I suppose) found the whites all right, and so they let them sleep there.*

Overall, the early encounters of Spanish explorers with the Tongva and other Native peoples were peaceful, with people offering food to the passing soldiers and the Spanish offering gifts of glass beads.

SPIRITUAL AND MILITARY CONQUEST

In Spain's frontier territories, colonial rulers had developed a three-pronged approach to settlement: the establishment of missions, presidios (forts) and pueblos (towns). The missions, as an arm of the Spanish crown in the conquering and colonizing of New Spain, were designed to convert Indigenous populations to the Catholic faith and create a colonial workforce, thus paving the way for settlers to establish towns.[43] Missions in Baja California had been established by the Dominican order;

however, Franciscans were tasked with the establishment of missions in Alta California.

Father Junípero Serra, at that time *presidente* of the Baja California missions, was appointed in 1769 to join Portolá and to lead a group of missionaries to Alta California. A statue of Serra, a well-known figure in California history, represents California in the statuary hall of the U.S. Capitol in Washington, D.C. The Capitol website describes Serra as "ascetic and uncompromising in his zeal to convert the Indians to Christianity."[44]

The conversion of Indigenous populations to the Catholic faith was a requirement established by the Spanish crown for colonization and was viewed as essential to save their souls from eternal damnation. In areas like Las Californias where the Indigenous population spanned numerous villages, it was necessary to bring the Indians together—by force if necessary—at central sites in a process referred to as *reducción* to make mass conversion easier. Hugo Reid, who lived at Mission San Gabriel in the 1840s, described one method of conversion. Soldiers or neophytes, Indigenous people newly converted to Catholic faith, would go to villages and persuade or force the people to come to the mission. Infants and children were baptized, and children over the age of eight were then kept apart from their parents. Mothers would accept baptism to be with their children, and men would be baptized in order to remain with their wives and children.[45]

Newly baptized converts were called *neófitas* (neophytes) to distinguish them from the unconverted *gentiles*. While the gentiles continued to live in their native villages, neófitas were required to reside and work at the missions in order to learn the skills necessary to ultimately become productive members of colonial society. Indigenous neófitas built the dormitories, church buildings, workshops, friars' rooms and military quarters at the missions. Married couples resided in their own huts; the unmarried youth slept in separate, sex-segregated dormitories. Girls between the ages of seven and nine were taken from their families to live in the *monjerío*, or dormitory for unmarried women, until they married. At night they were locked in under the supervision of an Indian mother. The boys slept in a separate dormitory. Conditions in the crowded and unsanitary dormitories, where the only toilet facilities in the locked room were a bucket or two, contributed to the rapid spread of diseases like measles that caused high death rates for mission Indians.[46]

According to Eulalia Pérez, the *llavera* (keyholder) at Mission San Gabriel responsible for the kitchens and food distribution, the neophytes ate together in the *pozolera*.[47] The pozolera was the dining hall, whose name comes from *pozole*, a hominy stew with meat and vegetables that was the common meal. Breakfast consisted of *atole*, or mush made of corn, barley or wheat, and occasionally *champurrado*, chocolate mixed with cornmeal gruel. For the noonday meal, pozole was served, with atole again for supper. These foods introduced by the friars were supplemented with nuts, seeds and other foods from the traditional Tongva diet when possible.[48]

The workday was strictly regulated. The day began with Mass, followed by breakfast and then an allotted task. Women might work at weaving cloth, blankets and sarapes or loading carts. Men would work as vaqueros (cowboys), either those who rode with saddles or those who rode bareback, or they might work tending the animals or in the fields. Other tasks included the making of wine, olive oil, soap, adobe bricks and leather items. The missions were designed to be self-sufficient communities, with workers engaged in tasks that were largely disconnected from their preconquest way of life. Workers received food, clothes and shelter but were not paid.

Initially, the California missions were to operate for ten years, after which time the church would remain as a parish church and the land would be distributed to the Indigenous workers.[49] In reality, the Franciscans opposed termination of the missions, arguing that the neófitas were not ready to live independently—apparently ignoring the fact that the Native peoples of California had been successfully living independently long before the arrival of the Spanish. Instead, the mission system continued in California for over fifty years. Twenty-one missions were established in Alta California between 1769 and 1823, and the system was not ended until secularization was completed by the Mexican government in 1834.

San Gabriel Arcángel, the fourth of the missions, was founded in 1771 on Tongva land by Father Serra. Through the process of *reducción*, different groups of Native peoples were brought together at a single mission. San Gabriel was home to the Tongva, Kitanemuk, Serrano and Cahuila people.[50] San Gabriel became a highly productive mission, with more than one hundred thousand head of cattle at its peak. The mission is credited with introducing large-scale viticulture to California and hence was one of Alta California's leading producers of wine grapes. The Spaniards gave the name gabrieleño, or Gabrielino, to the Native people of the San Gabriel Mission.[51] Currently, organizations representing the Tongva people make use of both the original and mission names.

The missions were typically served by two Franciscan friars plus a small detail of soldiers from the nearest presidio. Thus, all the work of constructing the buildings, raising livestock, planting and harvesting crops and producing

Ferdinand Deppe's painting *The Mission of San Gabriel, Alta California in May 1832* (1832), with Tongva families in foreground. *Collection of the Santa Bárbara Mission Archive Library. Gift of Daniel A. Hill.*

tools, food and clothing was done by Native labor. By Spanish law, the Native populations of the New World were free; however, the conditions of "free compulsory labor" under which they labored were not materially different from slavery.[52] For example, La Perouse, a French naval officer and head of a scientific expedition that visited California in 1786, stated that the conditions he observed at Mission San Carlos Borromeo reminded him of slave plantations in the West Indies. He described seeing "men and women loaded with irons, others in the stocks; and at length the noise of the strokes of a whip struck our ears."[53]

Numerous reports from foreign visitors, Spanish priests and mission Indians themselves document the physical punishments meted out at the missions for infringements of rules.[54] Flogging was common for a variety of infringements, including attempting to flee the mission, refusing to work, insolence and fornication. Soldiers and settlers were exempted from corporal punishment; corporal punishment, including flogging, was restricted to the Native population and was officially sanctioned by the friars as necessary for the correction of the neophytes.[55] Another punishment described by

Chumash Fernando Librado was the use of stocks. One type of stock was a sort of wooden shoe that was joined to a ring attached to the knee, with weights attached to the straps. Both men and women were forced to work in the fields wearing these weighted shoes.[56] Women who miscarried were also punished due to the assumption that they had tried to abort the fetuses they carried. Their punishment was flogging, accompanied by standing outside of the church for a given number of days holding a "hideously painted wooden child" in their arms.[57]

From the perspective of the Spanish priests, they were bringing spiritual salvation and the benefits of civilization to pagan people. They viewed discipline as necessary, in the same way that parents discipline their children, and they were dismayed by the high number of deaths that occurred at the missions. The goal of their work was the ultimate incorporation of the Indigenous populations into Catholic, Hispanic society, albeit on a level that was viewed as inferior to that of the Spanish. The consequences of the mission system, however, were disastrous for Indigenous peoples.

Toypurina

The establishment of ranchos such as Rancho Los Cerritos was done on lands that were contested. The workforce for the ranchos was created through coercive practices employed at the missions. The Tongva and other Native peoples did not accept the takeover of their lands by the Spanish and being forced to live and work at the missions without resistance. It is unlikely that the Native people fully understood that when they accepted baptism at the mission, in a language unknown to them, they were submitting to the unrelenting restrictions and harsh discipline of mission life. The goals of the mission system were not only to convert the Indigenous people to Christianity but also to acculturate them to Christian—that is, Hispanic—societal norms and practices. Their native culture was to be stamped out and replaced with Hispanic religion, language and culture.

Unsurprisingly, various Native groups made repeated attempts to resist Spanish encroachment on their land and to rebel against the missions. An early uprising against Mission San Gabriel was led by the Tongva shaman Toypurina and neophyte Nicolás José in 1785.

An early and oft-cited description of the uprising was written in 1958 by Thomas Workman Temple II, a genealogist among whose ancestors was the half-brother of a later owner of Rancho Los Cerritos. The author recalled first learning of Toypurina's plot from his mother, who had heard stories repeated by elders among her people. Temple later studied the Expediente, or official record of Toypurina's interrogation, which was made available to the public through the Archivo General de la Nación in Mexico City.[58]

Temple's melodramatic account of the uprising described Toypurina as a sorceress or witch who tempted Gabrielino warriors to engage in a "fiendish plot" to attack the mission by stating that she would use magic to kill the priests to initiate the rebellion. Writing several decades later, historian Steven Hackel stated that "largely because of Temple's article, Toypurina has become the symbol of Gabrielino resistance to the missions and an icon of California Indian women's resistance to colonial oppression."[59] Based on his investigations into mission records and the trial transcription, however, Hackel provides a more nuanced perspective on the uprising.

At the time of the rebellion, Mission San Gabriel had been in existence for fourteen years, and over 1,200 Indians (843 of them Gabrielinos) had been baptized there. Toypurina was a twenty-four-year-old shaman from the village of Japchivit, where her brother was a tomyaar, or chief. An unbaptized woman herself, she had been asked by Nicolás José to meet with tomyaars of other villages of unbaptized Indians in the area and to encourage them to join the rebellion. The attack was to take place on the first night of the new moon in October 1785. A young soldier stationed at the mission, José María Pico, overheard a conversation in which the plot was discussed. Pico had arrived with his family on the de Anza expedition of 1776 when he was seven years old and had learned the Tongva language growing up in Southern California.

When the corporal of the mission guard, José María Verdugo, learned of the plot, there was not time to send for reinforcements from the San Diego presidio. He devised a plan: two of his soldiers would impersonate priests, laid out on the floor of their dwelling as if in death, with black candles set at their heads, feet and sides. When the attacking Tongva warriors entered the room to observe the dead priests, the soldiers sprang up and, joined by the others, captured the warriors and Toypurina, who had accompanied them.

Twenty-one Gabrielinos were arrested, and the four rebel leaders were interrogated in the soldiers' quarters at the mission. A list of questions had been prepared by the governor of Alta California, Pedro Fages. The interrogation was carried out by Sergeant Olivera, with Fages and Verdugo as witnesses. Pico served as translator, and another soldier served as scribe

Mural featuring portrait of Toypurina in the Boyle Heights neighborhood of Los Angeles. *Courtesy of NPS/N Torres.*

to record the testimonies. The witnesses were exhorted to tell the truth or risk flogging. The two tomyaars who testified, Tomasajaquichi of the Juyuvit ranchería and Aliyivit of the Jajamovit ranchería, both identified Nicolás José and Toypurina as the instigators of the rebellion. When Toypurina testified, she stated that "she was angry with the Padres and with all of those of this Mission because [they] are living here in her land."[60] After two years of imprisonment, Toypurina was sent to live at the farthest mission possible from San Gabriel. She became a Christian and married Manuel Montero, a soldier from Puebla stationed at Mission San Carlos Borromeo, with whom she had four children.

Nicolás José testified that he had rebelled because neither the Franciscans nor the mission soldiers would permit the neophytes to engage in native dances or other traditional practices that the Spaniards termed "abuses" and saw as in conflict with Catholic beliefs. Although Temple's account cast Nicolás José as a braggart and troublemaker, mission records show that he was one of the first converts at the mission and was active in its affairs, serving as a witness at marriages and as a *padrino* (godfather) for numerous baptisms. He nonetheless attempted to maintain Gabrielino dances, rituals and celebrations and maintained contact with unbaptized Indians in surrounding villages. His faith in Catholicism may have been shaken by the deaths experienced by members of his village and his immediate family. One half of the fifty-four children of his village who were baptized died, including his own son, whose death was followed by that of his mother. After the military interrogation, Nicolás José was sentenced to six years of hard labor in irons at the most distant presidio from San Gabriel. His name does not recur in the colonial record.

Hackel interprets Toypurina's anger with "all of those of the mission" to have included not only the Spanish friars and soldiers but also the baptized Indians from Indigenous groups other than those closest to the mission. The increase in the mission population had been accomplished by bringing in others with whom the local villages had been in conflict prior to the arrival of the Spanish. The accompanying increase in agriculture and livestock on mission lands was endangering the existence of the villages of unbaptized Indians. Hackel concludes,

> *Indians like Nicolás José and Toypurina came from different villages and pursued different life paths, and both confronted the mission system and Spanish colonization. Yet each found something different to fear in the colonial order. For Nicolás José, the Gabrielino from Sibapet and baptized Indian of the mission, it was the threat the missionaries, soldiers, and disease posed to Gabrielino culture that led to rebellion; while for Toypurina, the unbaptized "wise" woman from Japchivit, it was the threat the relocated coastal Gabrielinos and other Indians at the expanding mission posed to the native subsistence economy and political order that prompted the attack on the mission.*[61]

Continuing Resistance

The uprising at San Gabriel by the Tongva was one of the first times that Indigenous people rebelled against the mission system and its impact on their lives and culture, but it was by no means the only one.[62] The largest rebellion took place in 1824, when Chumash Indians from three missions (Santa Bárbara, Santa Inés and La Purísima Concepción) rose up. In anticipation of attacks by the pirate Bouchard in 1818, Father Ripoll of Mission Santa Barbara had armed and trained a contingent of 180 Indigenous troops. Father Payeras at La Purísima formed a similar company. These troops, trained in the weapons and tactics of European warfare, were instrumental in the uprisings, which were organized to occur simultaneously at the three missions. After initial Chumash successes, soldiers regained control of the missions and were sent in pursuit of the

Indians who had escaped to relocate in the *tulares*, regions in the Central Valley where tule (bulrush) grows. Several military patrols were sent out, and some of the Indians were captured and persuaded to return to mission life.[63]

There are numerous accounts of Native peoples resisting mission life by fleeing the missions; their reasons for flight were captured in the interrogations carried out when they were recaptured.[64] Their reasons included seeking to escape whippings, incarceration in the stocks or dying of hunger. It has been estimated that one in twenty-four neophytes successfully fled the mission system.[65] Native resistance to mission life also took more covert forms, such as maintaining cultural practices in secret. Stories and family histories continued to be communicated orally outside of the presence of mission fathers and soldiers.

Indigenous people sought to push the invaders out of their land or flee to the interior of the state to escape Spanish rule. Even the gentiles, those who were able to evade mission life and continue to live in their native villages, experienced disruption to their lifeways from the ecological changes that accompanied farming and large-scale animal husbandry at the missions. Many of the gentiles resorted to seeking work at the ranchos or in towns where they were not pressured to convert to Catholicism and were able to retain some of their traditional practices.

Impact of the Missions

A major impact of conquest and mission settlement was demographic in nature. Between 1769 and the end of Mexican rule in 1846, California's Indian population declined by more than half, from approximately 310,000 to approximately 150,000. Most of the Indigenous deaths were due to diseases that accompanied European settlement for which they lacked natural immunity—malaria, smallpox, yellow fever, measles and cholera. Syphilis, also introduced by Europeans, took a toll by weakening the constitutions of the afflicted, making them more susceptible to other diseases.[66]

The reducción and concentration of Indians at the missions—crowded in dormitories, living in insalubrious conditions and fed an unfamiliar and often insufficient diet—augmented the spread and effects of these diseases. It has been estimated that one in three infants born at the missions died before reaching their first birthday. Currently the term *continuous traumatic stress* is used to describe the psychological impact of living in conditions in which there is a continuous and real threat of danger. This most likely applies to the Indigenous survivors of disease and the conditions of mission life. Historian Elias Castillo contends that depression, malnourishment and disease not only weakened the mission Indians physically but also "instilled in them a sense of hopelessness."[67]

According to Tongva cultural educator Craig Torres, some Indigenous families passed down oral stories regarding their ancestors' experiences: "You would hear these stories all the time, and it was just repetition, repetition, repetition, repetition, and because of the repetition I think I can really recall all those stories in exactly the way it was said."[68] Torres added, however, that this was not the case with other families. Many families chose not to pass on stories and cultural experiences to their children and grandchildren. "I know that people were always reluctant to pass things down because it was a way of erasing that memory of your family that was so tragic and…the trauma that was associated with it that people didn't want to [remember]."

The mission system was devised with the explicit goal of replacing Indigenous spiritual beliefs and practices with the Catholic religion. This was to be accomplished within a broader process of acculturation to Hispanic social norms and lifestyle, accompanied by the abandonment of traditional practices deemed antithetical to Christianity, such as nudity, infanticide, belief in the powers of shamans and use of hallucinogenic drugs.[69] The native languages were to be replaced with the Spanish language and native names with Spanish ones at baptism. A second major impact of the mission system was thus cultural assault.

A third major consequence was ecological. Individuals or villages who were able to resist incorporation into the mission system found it increasingly difficult to maintain their traditional way of life due to the destruction of native habitats associated with large-scale raising of cattle and agriculture. Pastures that had been tended for centuries with the purpose of enhancing the grasses and shrubs that were fed upon by deer, antelope and small game were destroyed. Traditional lands that had furnished acorns, berries and seeds were now occupied by others, and the land was being put to other uses.

Coastal tribes such as the Tongva experienced forced assimilation to Spanish colonial society to a greater extent than tribes in the northern and interior regions of California due to the desirability of their lands (such as the

Los Angeles Basin) for ranching, farming and harbors and their accessibility by sea. In his book *Indians of California: The Changing Image*, historian James Rawls sums up the impact of the missions and the subsequent consequences for ranchos such as Rancho Los Cerritos as follows:

> *Although the missionaries intended to prepare the Indians for self-sufficiency within the colonial society, in fact they prepared them for severe and extensive exploitation once the missions were disbanded. As the missions neared their end, the released neophytes were much sought after by Mexican rancheros, who viewed them as a potentially valuable supply of labor.*[70]

CHAPTER 2

ROOTS OF THE RANCHO

The site that would become Rancho Los Cerritos began as part of a large concession of land granted by the Spanish crown to Manuel Nieto, a loyal soldier in the frontier territory of Alta California. The grant was divided among his children after his death, and title to the section called Los Cerritos was later validated by the Mexican government. Thus, the history of the Rancho spans the period in which California was part of a Spanish colony through its inclusion in the country of Mexico after Mexico's independence from Spain and into the period in which California became the thirty-first state of the United States.

Soldiers and the Presidios

The establishment of the missions and the subsequent impact on Indigenous Tongva culture and life are described in chapter 1. In the Spanish colonial plan, presidios (forts) housed the soldiers tasked with protecting the missions and settlers from rebellions of the Native population as well as from foreign attack. Four presidios were ultimately established along the California coast at San Diego, Santa Barbara, Monterey, and San Francisco. A small group of soldiers from the presidio closest to each mission was assigned to work and reside at the mission.

Soldado de cuera with leather jacket, bull-hide shield and lance. *Public domain.*

Leather-jacket soldiers, or *soldados de cuera*, such as those accompanying Gaspar de Portolá and serving at the presidios, received their name from the leather jacket (*cuera*) made from five to seven layers of deerskin that they wore for protection against arrows. These mounted soldiers, or dragoons, carried a leather shield and lance and were noted for their horsemanship. Many who came to Alta California had previously served in frontier garrisons in Baja California and the northern territories of Sonora and Sinaloa. One of the soldiers on the Portolá expedition was Manuel Nieto, who would later be granted the lands that included Rancho Los Cerritos.

MANUEL NIETO

Manuel Nieto (1734–1804) was born in La Villa de Sinaloa in present-day Mexico. Recruitment of soldiers for service in Alta California in what are now the northern territories of Mexico was heavy, and several of Nieto's comrades-in-arms hailed from the same town. Nieto arrived in Alta California as part of Portolá's expedition but did not stay. He later returned as part of the de Anza expedition, the first colonizing expedition to Alta California. Soldiers accompanied the group of settlers, which included several women who gave birth along the route, traveling from the Tubac presidio in northwestern Mexico to arrive at the presidio of Monterey in 1776. Among the settlers making the trek as part of the expedition was a widow with two girls aged six and four.

Later, a group of settlers was recruited largely from Sonora and Sinaloa to establish a second pueblo, the Pueblo de Nuestra Señora de Los Ángeles de Porciúncula (present-day Los Angeles). Enticements offered to future settlers included an annual salary, land for a *solar* (home) and a *suerte* (garden plot) and access to communal lands for grazing livestock.[71] Because of the large number of animals accompanying the settlers—a herd of over one thousand horses, mules, goats and sheep—the expedition, led by Captain Rivera y Moncada, followed the overland route previously opened by de Anza. Although most of the settlers made it safely to Southern California, Rivera y Moncada and many of his soldiers were killed along with the local missionaries at Mission San Pedro y San Pablo de Bicuñeon on the Colorado River during an uprising of the Quechan Indians.

The original group of *pobladores*, or settlers, was made up of twelve families and included experienced farmers, laborers, miners and at least two artisans. Ethnically, the group was representative of northern Mexico, being made up of people with Indigenous, African and European ancestry.[72] All the adults had been born in Mexico with the exception of a Filipino from the Spanish colony of the Philippines and a Spaniard from Cádiz. The expedition first arrived at Mission San Gabriel in 1781 and later made its way to a site near the Tongva village of Yaang'na (Iyáangá in the Tongva language) to establish the pueblo.

The survival and success of the nascent pueblo depended greatly on the presence of a nearby and prosperous Tongva village, located by the freshwater artesian aquifer of the Los Angeles River. The pobladores, with their experience farming in the semiarid lands of northern Mexico, made a priority of digging the *zanja*, a system of irrigation ditches to carry water from the Los Angeles River to their garden plots.[73] The settlers relied on Indigenous labor provided by gentiles, or unbaptized Indians not associated with the mission. Indigenous workers planted and harvested wheat and corn, maintained the zanja and worked as household servants, grinding corn, cooking and washing clothes.[74]

Manuel Nieto was a soldado de cuera attached to the San Diego garrison. Spanish colonial bureaucracy produced detailed reports that were sent to Spain and archived in the Archivo General de Indias in Sevilla, Spain. The 1790 census of the garrison at San Diego, for example, includes the name, age, birthplace, race, and accompanying family members of all eight officers and forty-nine soldiers who formed the garrison. Among these is the soldado de cuera Manuel Pérez Nieto. He is listed as a fifty-six-year-old *mulato* from the territory of Sinaloa, who was accompanied by his wife, Maria Teresa Morillo, from Loreto, Baja California; their two children; and Nieto's mother, Manuela Pérez, aged seventy.

A word should be said about the racial identities of the early soldiers and settlers of Alta California. Although they are often referred to as Spanish soldiers and the period as one of Spanish settlement, the term *Spanish* can be misleading when referring to individuals. Very few of the original settlers, such as those who established Los Angeles or the soldiers in the various presidios, were born in Spain. The majority were born in New Spain, and most, although possessing some Spanish ancestry, were actually bi- or multiracial.[75] Manuel Nieto's race was listed in garrison records as mulato: that is, mixed Spanish and Black, or Afro-Latino in present-day usage. In the San Diego garrison, fourteen of the fifty-seven soldiers were of mixed African heritage, listed either as *mulato* or *color quebrado*. Among the other soldiers were *mestizos*, or mixed Spanish and Indigenous; *coyotes*, or mixed-race with more Indigenous background; and *Indios*, or Indigenous people. The majority of the soldiers, thirty-four of the fifty-seven, were listed as *español*, or Spanish, but only two of these men were born in Spain.

The term *español*, as it was used in Alta California, denoted a person with at least some Spanish heritage. As a term of social identity, it denoted social status more than race and was somewhat fluid; it was possible for a person's identity to shift over time with changes in social status through the accumulation of land and wealth. A person might be listed as a mestizo in one census and as an español in a later census. Such a change in racial identity over time is seen in the case of José María Pico. Although he was listed in a 1790 garrison census as an español, he had brothers who were mulatos at Santa Barbara and Los Angeles, while his parents, who lived in Los Angeles, were listed as a mestizo and a mulata.[76] Use of the term *español*, and particularly its translation as "Spaniard," resulted in the misleading practice of later chroniclers and historians referring to soldiers in Alta California as "pure-blooded Spanish" or of "good Spanish blood." This practice obscured the multiracial reality of early California society.

For mixed-race individuals in frontier territories, military service offered an opportunity for social and economic advancement. Service in California, the farthest and last of the frontier territories of New Spain, brought the promise of land for settlement upon retirement from the army. Some of the founders of landowning *ranchero* families who became the elite in Alta California, such as Pico, Yorba, Verdugo, Sepúlveda, Féliz and Cota, were among the soldiers of the San Diego garrison.

Soldiers at the Missions

The full contingent of approximately sixty officers and soldiers was rarely found at a presidio. It was common for a detachment of six or seven soldiers forming an *escolta* to be sent from a presidio garrison to serve at one of the surrounding missions. Manuel Nieto was part of the escolta at Mission San Gabriel. The duties of the soldiers at the missions included policing the mission area, transporting supplies and accompanying the friars on their visits to the villages of Indigenous neophytes.[77] Unmarried soldiers were housed in barracks, while married soldiers, who often took their families with them when assigned to mission duty, received individual rooms. The wives assisted the missionaries in instructing neophytes in the domestic arts of sewing, weaving, cooking and grinding corn.[78] Juana Machado, the wife of one of the soldiers serving with Manuel Nieto, described how the wives who were pregnant would return to the presidio when the time approached to give birth.[79] Resident soldiers were permitted to acquire their own cattle, which could graze along with mission cattle on the mission lands.[80]

Soldiers' duties included protecting the mission from attacks by non-Christianized Indians continuing to live outside of the missions as well as forming search parties to bring back neophytes who sought to escape from repressive mission living conditions. There was not, however, protection of the Indians from the soldiers themselves. Mission friars continually complained about soldiers' mistreatment of Indigenous people and particularly the rape of Native women, a common occurrence. Historian Miroslava Chávez-García interprets the widespread sexual violence against women, stating, "In a patriarchal and ethnically stratified society that devalued females and non-Europeans, native women occupied the lowest rung of society and were treated as the spoils of war."[81]

Treatment by the soldiers as well as the harsh discipline of the mission friars led to uprisings on the part of the Indigenous people. One of the rebellions in which Manuel Nieto played a role was that of the Tongva leader Toypurina at Mission San Gabriel in 1785 (described in chapter 1).

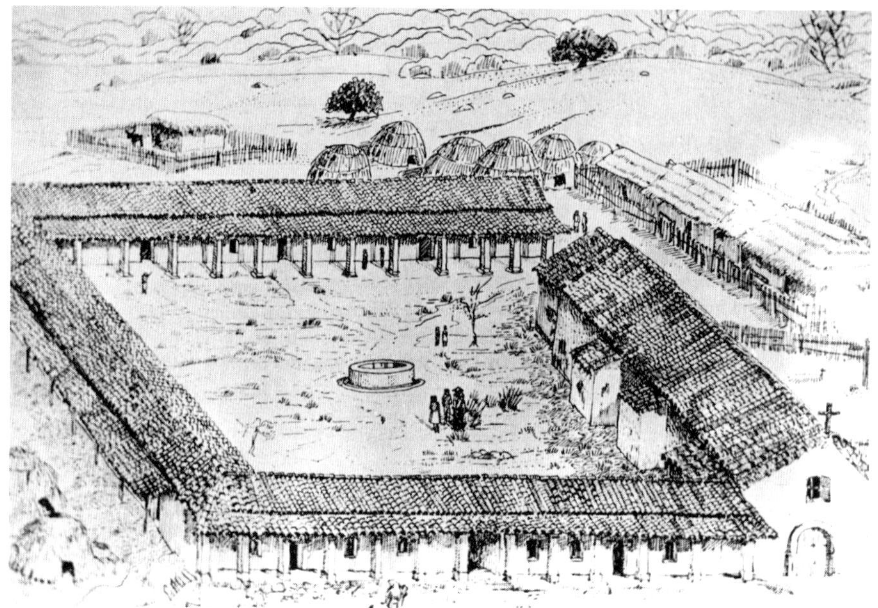

Santa Barbara presidio. *Gledhill Library, Santa Barbara Historical Museum.*

Nieto and Juan José Domínguez were the soldiers chosen by Corporal of the Guard José María Verdugo to impersonate friars and pretend to be laid out in death. When the Tongva warriors arrived, the soldiers reportedly leapt into action with the cry, "Santiago!"[82] Santiago, or Saint James, was the patron saint of the *reconquista*, or the reconquest of Moorish Spain by Christian forces, and "Santiago y Cierra España" was the troops' war cry. In Spain he was referred to as Santiago Matamoros, or St. James the Moor Slayer. In the New World, he became known as Santiago Mataindios, or St. James the Indian Slayer.

Original Land Concession

The Spanish crown sought to regulate social, political, religious and economic life in its widespread empire, particularly regarding the interaction between settlers and Indigenous peoples, through a series of laws and decrees that made up the Leyes de las Indias, or Laws of the Indies. Although the Laws of the Indies provided for the granting of concessions of one square league (approximately four acres) to grantees for the raising of livestock, large grants of land were typically not made to individual citizens in the colonial period. Rather, most of the desirable land for farming and the raising of livestock was held by the missions.

A limited number of land concessions were granted permitting use of the land for raising livestock, with title to real property vested solely in the Crown. These concessions were intended to be provisional in nature and did not convey rights of ownership. In fact, no deeds to land title were issued by the Spanish government. It would later prove to be problematic for longtime residents and their heirs to establish ownership of these early grants.

In 1773, the viceroy authorized allotments of land to be made adjacent to the presidios at San Diego and Monterey. A small grant of land made to Manuel Butrón, a Monterey soldier, was the first such grant in Alta California. His parcel of less than one hundred acres was abandoned a few years later. Subsequently, royal orders changed, permitting the granting of larger parcels of land than those that had previously been authorized in the Provincias Internas (northwestern Mexico plus Baja and Alta California).

Under these new guidelines, in 1784, Governor Pedro Fages received petitions for land from three soldiers who had served in the province since the Portolá expedition. The process they followed was relatively simple: petitioners addressed a letter to the governor describing the land they requested, and he gave his endorsement in a note on the margins of the petition itself. Fages granted sixteen square leagues (over seventy-five thousand acres) to Juan José Domínguez for what became known as Rancho San Pedro, and the thirty-six-thousand-acre parcel known as Rancho San Rafael was granted to José María Verdugo. The largest parcel, initially three hundred thousand acres, was granted to Manuel Nieto and became known as Rancho Los Nietos. In his endorsement of Nieto's petition, Governor Fages wrote,

> *San Gabriel, October 21, 1784. I grant the petitioner the permission of having the bovine stock and horses at the place of La Zanja or its environs, provided no harm is done to the Mission San Gabriel, nor to the pagan Indians of its environs in any manner whatsoever; and that he must have someone to watch it, and to go and sleep at the aforementioned Pueblo. Pedro Fages.*[83]

Since Nieto could not read nor write, it is likely that he had a corporal prepare the land petition for him, and he signed with the mark of a cross.[84] The three parcels granted to Domínguez, Verdugo and Nieto were thus the first large rancho grants made in Alta California. Rancho Los Nietos would later be subdivided, with one twenty-seven-thousand-acre section becoming Rancho Los Cerritos.

Descriptions in the land petitions were imprecise, relying not on measurement of the parcel but rather on the identification of physical characteristics to mark boundaries. This practice fueled ongoing litigation by rancheros (ranch owners) over disputed boundaries. Manuel Nieto was involved in a lengthy controversy with his former comrade-in-arms, Juan José Dominguez of Rancho San Pedro. Nieto's land bordered Rancho San Pedro along the Los Angeles River. Because the river's year-round flow was so erratic, it was never able to dig a definite channel for itself and changed course often. At times, it did not empty into San Pedro Bay as it currently does but rather flowed into Santa Monica Bay along the present course of Ballona Creek.[85] Over time, the boundary between the two ranchos changed as much as a half mile in either direction. This resulted in the cattle of one rancho grazing on land now belonging to the other rancho, and their calves being branded by vaqueros (cowboys) of the other rancho. This dispute continued and was not settled until long after the death of the two original rancheros.

The size of the 300,000-acre grant to Manuel Nieto was unusual for the time. Rancho Los Nietos was located southwest of Mission San Gabriel, between the San Gabriel foothills to the north, the Los Angeles River to the west, the Santa Ana River to the east and the Pacific Ocean to the south. After a dispute with Mission San Gabriel in 1790, however, the northern portion of the original grant was awarded to the mission, reducing Nieto's rancho to 167,000 acres. Still immense, this land grant included the present-day cities of Long Beach, Lakewood, Bellflower, Signal Hill, Downey, Norwalk, Santa Fe Springs, Whittier, Artesia, Westminster, Garden Grove, Huntington Beach and Fountain Valley.

Although Nieto received the land grant in 1784, he initially remained in the army and was stationed at Mission San Gabriel. A requirement for receiving a grant of land was constructing a home on the property, which Nieto proceeded to do. His home was made of sun-dried adobe bricks. The term *adobe* was used to refer to both the material that the bricks were made of (mud mixed with straw) and a house made of adobe. Typical adobe homes of the period were twenty by forty-one feet, a single story in height, with a packed dirt floor and a wide porch. The adobe was divided into two rooms, one of which served as the *sala* or living room. Cooking was done in a partially roofed area outside the building.[86] Nails were not used, and the roof beams were lashed together with rawhide strips. The strips would shrink and stretch according to the weather, causing them to creak and groan at night.[87] Nieto's adobe was located near the present-day city of Whittier.

After Nieto's death in 1804, his widow continued living at the rancho. Rancho Los Nietos was divided informally among his children: his daughter and widows of his sons as well as his son Juan José received parcels. The land titles were subsequently formalized by Governor José Figueroa in 1834. By then, the process of validating earlier colonial land claims by the Mexican government was a more formalized procedure requiring quantitative measurement of the land. This was done by *cordeleros*, or cord bearers, who used cords of fifty or one hundred *varas* in length (one vara was equal to thirty-three inches) with a stake at each end. Horsemen would plant the stake and ride until the cord ended to plant a second stake at the other end.

A ceremony of receiving land that was common in Mexican California and was documented for Rancho Cucamonga may have been performed by the Nieto heirs as well. At Rancho Cucamonga, following receipt of the official proclamation of possession by the officer in charge,

> *The grantee demonstrated his acceptance of and dominion over the premises by walking over the same and throwing grass and stones to the four winds of heaven. This ceremony—so like the ancient sign of our Saxon ancestors is regarded by us as useless—the performance of which secured his rights and omission of which defeated the title. Not so! Said the Land Commission. It would have nothing to do with what it considered folk nonsense.*[88]

The 28,000-acre Rancho Los Alamitos and 48,800-acre Rancho Los Coyotes went to Juan José Nieto. Antonio María Nieto's widow, María Josefa Cota de Nieto, received the 17,600-acre Rancho Santa Gertrudes. The widow of José Antonio Nieto, Catarina Ruíz de Nieto, received the 33,400-acre Rancho Las Bolsas. Nieto's daughter Manuela Nieto de Cota inherited the 27,000-acre parcel called Los Cerritos, or "little hills."[89] Interestingly, after approval of partition of the land, Governor Figueroa was able to purchase Rancho Los Alamitos from Juan José Nieto for a mere $500. Perhaps the low price was intended to spur the governor's approval of the secularization of mission lands, a process that released these vast lands for acquisition by individual rancheros.[90] The governor, now a landowning ranchero himself, subsequently approved the legislature's plan for secularization.

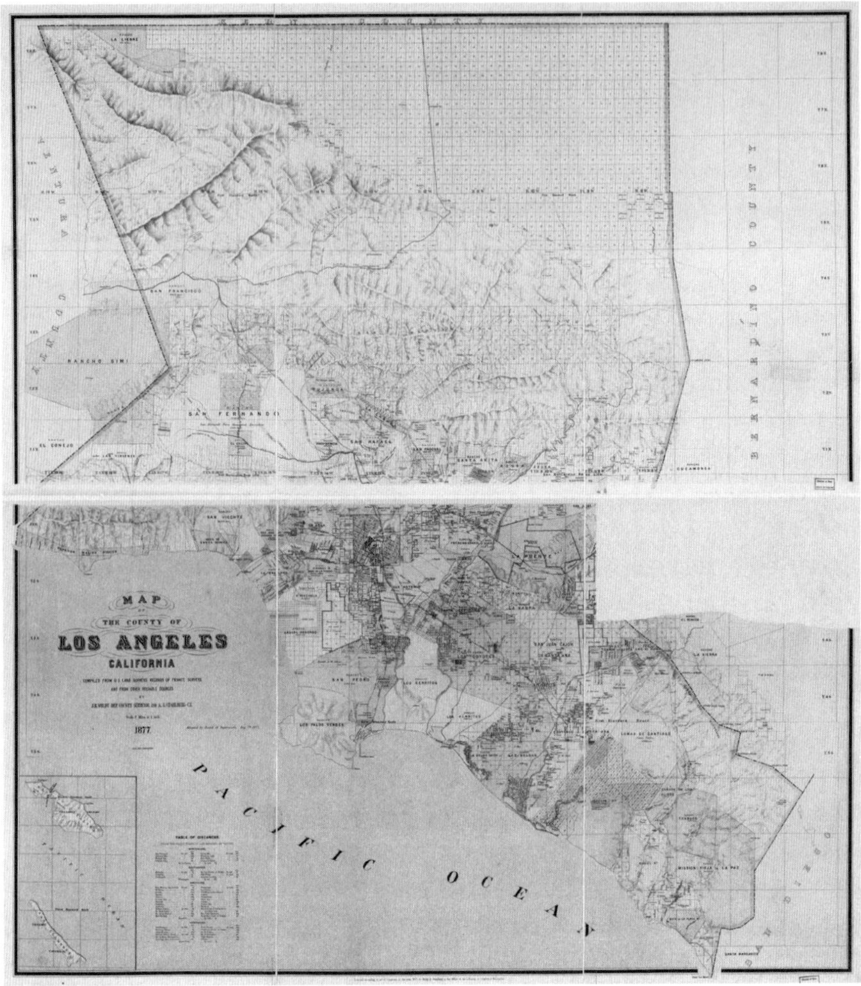

Map of the ranchos making up the original Nieto land grant with current cities. *Library of Congress, Geography and Maps Division.*

Mexican Rule

Manuel Nieto died before Spanish rule of California ended with Mexican independence in 1821. California's distance from the capital and the difficulty of travel caused a yearlong delay before Californios received news of independence. A soldier's wife described the simple ceremony that marked independence at the Presidio of San Diego.

There was no flag pole. A corporal or soldier held the Spanish flag in one hand and the Mexican flag in the other. Both of the flags were attached to little sticks. In the presence of Officer Don José María Estudillo, Commander Ruíz gave the cry "Long live the Mexican empire!" Then the Mexican flag was raised amidst salvos of artillery and fusillade.[91]

The next day, the soldiers were ordered to cut off their braids, symbolizing the severing of service to the Crown. Soldiers had been accustomed to wearing their hair in long braids tied with a ribbon or silk knot. Although most of the soldiers swore allegiance to Mexico, a few did not, and many soldiers and settlers continued to think of themselves as Californios rather than *mexicanos*.

Mexican independence had profound implications for life in Alta California. Under Spanish colonial rule, commerce was restricted to trade with the mother country and ports were not open to foreign ships. The opening of the ports of Monterey, Santa Barbara and San Diego to foreign trade brought not only goods not formerly available but American and European traders and businessmen as well. One of these was John Temple, the future owner of Rancho Los Cerritos.

The ruling to secularize the missions in 1834 further transformed California society. The missions had been established in accordance with the Laws of the Indies that regulated Spain's colonies in the Americas. Mission lands were to be held in trust and then returned to the Indigenous converts once they had accepted Christianity and learned trades useful in colonial society and were prepared to take their place as independent settlers themselves. The codes of Recopilación stated that the frontier missions were to have a life of not more than ten years.[92] With secularization came the opportunity for Indigenous receipt of land. However, with few exceptions, this did not occur. Rather, mission lands were made available for sale—thus the granting of approximately six hundred rancho titles by Mexican governors. Dispossession of mission lands resulted in a labor force of landless Indigenous workers who were then hired as vaqueros and ranch workers or as laborers who sought work in the pueblos.

Currently, the term *rancho* has several different definitions in Latin America. It can be the English-language equivalent of *ranch*, or land used for the raising of livestock. In Mexico it often refers to a rural village. It may also be used to refer to a poor and precarious dwelling. In early California, during the Spanish and Mexican periods of California history, the term *rancho* referred to a tract of land used for raising livestock with an occupied home.

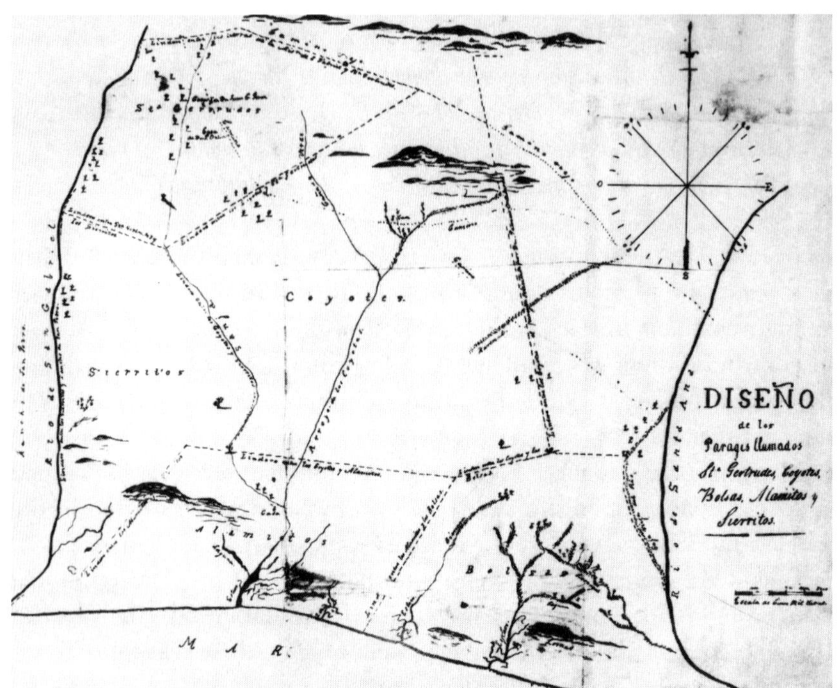

Hand-drawn diseño of Rancho Los Cerritos and the other ranchos on Rancho Los Nietos land, surveyed by Abel Stearns. *Rancho Los Cerritos Collection.*

Ranchos were acquired as either a land grant or a land concession (right to use without actual ownership of the land) from the government for cattle ranching. Although the stereotypical ranchero is a member of the wealthy elite who owns a large tract of land, in actuality ranchos were of different sizes, and relatively few were the size of those inherited by Nieto heirs.[93]

Although the Nieto family had agreed informally on the distribution of Rancho Los Nietos lands among the siblings, formal titles were not granted until 1834. The process established that year by the Mexican government required a formal letter of petition to the corresponding local official (*alcalde* or prefect), followed by the *informe* or document stating approval of the grant. The petition and informe were sent along with a *diseño* to the governor for filing in the archives.[94] The diseños were hand-drawn maps that included the landmarks that formed the boundaries of the parcel of land, often a river, a zanja or canal, a rock formation or a tree. The diseño for the Los Nietos ranchos was done by Abel Stearns. The lack of precision in many of the diseños would cause problems later when validation of the titles with American courts was required.

Californio Society

Manuel Nieto's daughter, Manuela Nieto de Cota, and her husband, Guillermo, were *hijos del país* (literally "children of the country"), a term for settler descendants born in Alta California. Hijos del país were a racially mixed group that included those considered españoles, mestizos and mulatos. Historian Rosaura Sánchez notes, however, that in California, multiple social categories were concentrated in the distinction between *gente de razón* and local Indians, which was essentially a cultural one. *Gente de razón*—literally "people of reason"—referred to the Californio, non-Indian population. According to Sánchez, the gente de razón over time "downplayed (and forgot) their own mixed heritages and saw themselves as *españoles*."[95]

The term *of reason* needs to be understood in contrast to its opposite: *sin razón*, or without reason. The concept was originally proposed during the Spanish Inquisition to release Indigenous peoples from culpability for heretical actions because of their presumed inability to distinguish right from wrong with regard to theology. Monroy explains,

> *Positively defined in Mexican California, the phrase* gente de razón *came to refer to anyone who was Catholic, Spanish-speaking, and who renounced instinctual behavior in favor of service to work, community, and the Crown. Negatively, it came to contrast a resident of California with anyone who behaved like an "Indian," or how an Indian was imagined to be.*[96]

The missions were intended to serve as institutions to teach the Catholic faith, the Spanish language and the skills and attitudes of Hispanic society. In other words, they were to foster Indians into the category of gente de razón. While this might have been achieved in some individual cases, the system retained most neophytes in conditions of forced labor and residence, considered "children" by the friars and thus not ready to take their place in colonial society.

Increasingly, gente de razón considered themselves Californios—that is, people of Spanish heritage who were born in California or who settled there during the Mexican era.[97] California was their *patria*, or homeland, and after independence, Mexico was seen as a distant and foreign place. Californios sought some control over policies in their territory, repeatedly rebelling against governors sent from the central government who were not hijos del país. They made the distinction between themselves and mexicanos, more recent immigrants born in Mexico.

At the time that Manuela Nieto and her siblings had their rancho titles validated under Mexican governmental regulations, the secularization of the missions was happening simultaneously, and many Californios were awarded mission lands—lands that had been appropriated from the original Indigenous people. Rancho owners took advantage of an Indigenous labor force that had been forcibly created at the missions and was now displaced from mission lands to provide needed labor for their ranchos. The exploitation of Indigenous labor was justified in the eyes of Californios using the distinction, and value judgment, of gente de razón versus gente sin razón.

Manuela Nieto de Cota

Manuela Nieto and her husband, Guillermo Cota, raised twelve children at Rancho Los Cerritos. They built an adobe home on the property, near where the RLC Visitor Center is currently located. Manuela's husband, Juan Ignacio Guillermo Cota, was born in Loreto, Baja California. He was the son and nephew of Roque and Antonio Cota, who had accompanied the de Anza expedition in the founding of the pueblo of Los Angeles. Guillermo Cota was a leading citizen of Los Angeles, serving as a *comisionado* of the pueblo and later mayor. One of Cota's duties as military commissioner was the establishment of estate boundaries when these were under dispute, riding out in the company of the mayor and *regidores* to lay out boundaries.

Although cattle ranching was the mainstay of Alta California's economy and the main activity at Rancho Los Cerritos, corn and wheat were also raised. As the ranchero, or ranch owner, Guillermo would have spent most of the day in the saddle, looking over his herds, inspecting range and water conditions or visiting neighboring rancheros. Californios—rancheros and vaqueros alike—were famed for their horsemanship. Indigenous laborers worked as vaqueros, sheepherders, household servants and cooks.

Manuela would have been responsible for supervising Indigenous household staff in the domestic chores of grinding corn, cooking, weaving, sewing, cleaning and doing laundry.[98] Native women baked in *hornos* (adobe ovens) heated by wood they had gathered. They washed clothes by scrubbing them against stones in the river, carded wool and sewed clothes by hand. With few doctors in the territory, women in childbirth were assisted by other

Cota adobe built circa 1835, as it appeared circa 1918. *Rancho Los Cerritos Collection.*

women.[99] Meals for the ranchero family consisted of hot chocolate, bread, tortillas and porridge for breakfast and meat with chilis, onions, tomatoes and beans later in the day. Workers had milk or water with *pinole* (parched corn) for breakfast and beans with tortillas for the evening meal.[100]

Most of the workers on ranchos such as Manuela Nieto de Cota's were Indigenous people. Up to the mid-1830s (that is, prior to the secularization of the missions), the majority of the rancho workers were gentiles, or non-mission Indians. They lived in rude huts and were provided food; in some cases, they received pay for their labor. They were not required to convert to Catholicism and continued to engage in traditional subsistence activities such as harvesting wild seeds.[101]

During the Spanish period, Manuela Nieto de Cota was the only woman to obtain property when, after the death of her father, the Los Nietos rancho was divided among Manuela and her brothers, José Antonio, Antonio María and Juan José. Later, at the time of the official granting of land titles during the Mexican period, her title was confirmed, as were the rights of her sisters-in-law, widows of José Antonio and Antonio María who inherited Ranchos Santa Gertrudes and Las Bolsas. In Mexican California, landownership by women was not uncommon. In Los Angeles in the 1830s and 1840s, there were twenty-seven *rancheras*, or female landowners, and ten were wealthy enough to own a second home in the pueblo.[102]

Manuela passed away in 1837, and in 1843, her children sold Rancho Los Cerritos to New Englander John Temple for $3,000 (equivalent to approximately $110,850 today). Temple paid an additional $25 for rights to

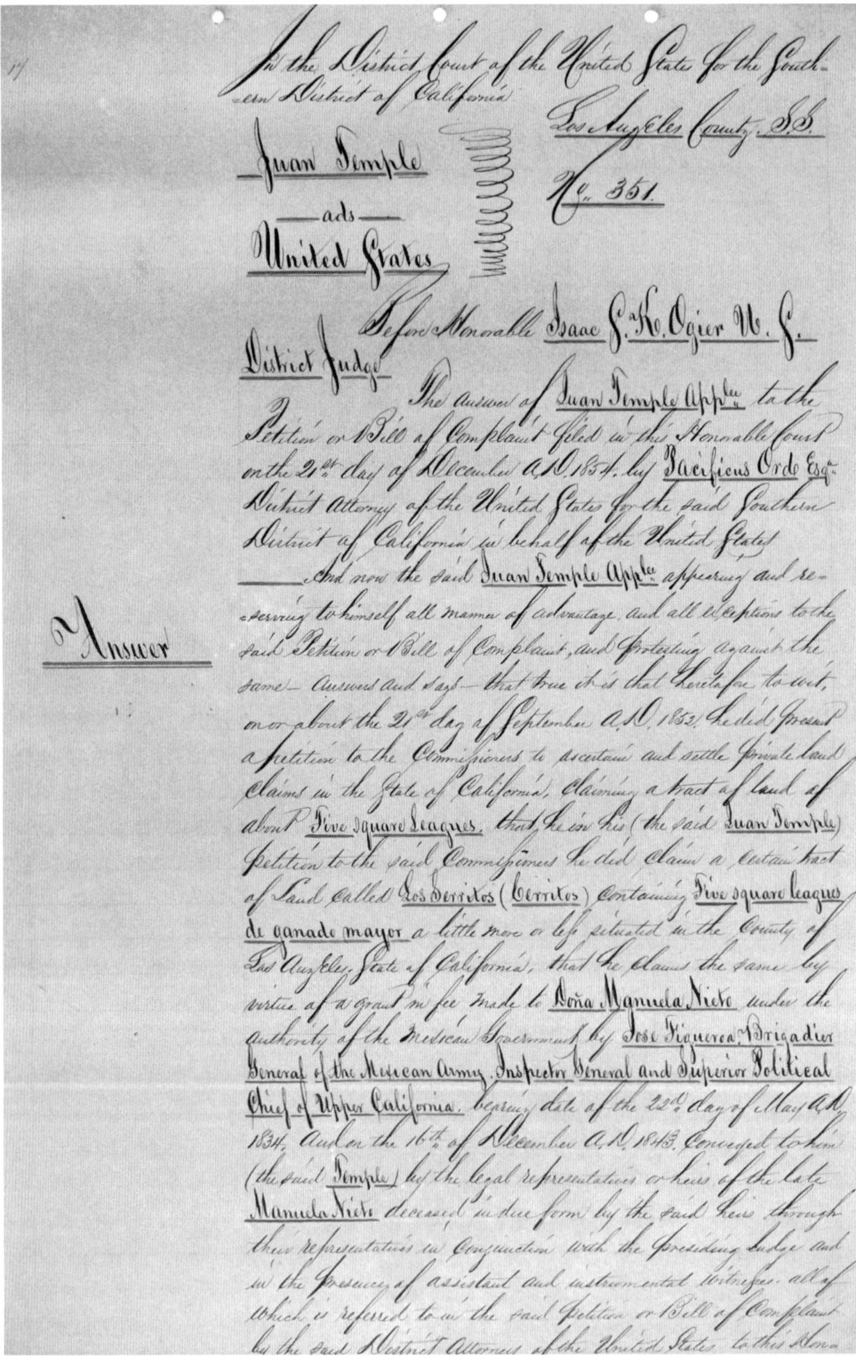

17

In the District Court of the United States for the South-ern District of California

Los Angeles County, S.S.

Juan Temple
ads
United States

No. 351.

Before Honorable Isaac S. K. Ogier U. S. District Judge

The answer of Juan Temple Applee to the Petition or Bill of Complaint filed in this Honorable Court on the 21st day of December A.D. 1854, by Pacificus Ord Esqr. District Attorney of the United States for the said Southern District of California in behalf of the United States

Answer

And now the said Juan Temple Applee appearing and reserving to himself all manner of advantage and all exceptions to the said Petition or Bill of Complaint, and protesting against the same— Answers and says— that true it is that heretofore to wit, on or about the 21st day of September A.D. 1852, he did present a petition to the Commissioners to ascertain and settle private land claims in the State of California, claiming a tract of land of about Five square Leagues, that he in his (the said Juan Temple) petition to the said Commissioners he did claim a certain tract of land called Los Serritos (Cerritos) containing Five square leagues de ganado mayor a little more or less situated in the County of Los Angeles, State of California, that he claims the same by virtue of a grant in fee made to Doña Manuela Nieto under the authority of the Mexican Government by Jose Figueroa, Brigadier General of the Mexican Army, Inspector General and Superior Political Chief of Upper California, bearing date of the 22nd day of May A.D. 1834, and on the 16th of December A.D. 1843, conveyed to him (the said Temple) by the legal representatives or heirs of the late Manuela Nieto deceased in due form by the said heirs through their representatives in conjunction with the presiding Judge and in the presence of assistant and instrumental witnesses, all of which is referred to in the said Petition or Bill of Complaint by the said District Attorney of the United States to this Hon-

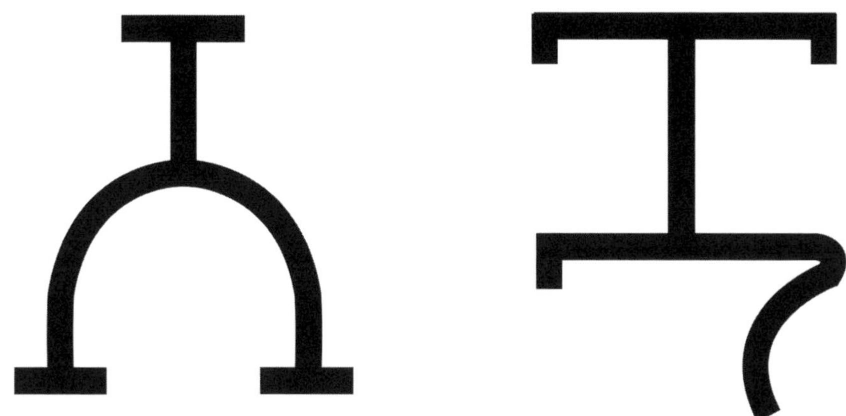

Opposite: Signature page from the Temple title appeal document showing sale by Manuela Nieto de Cota's heirs to John Temple. *Rancho Los Cerritos Collection.*

Above: The Nieto brand (*left*) was purchased by Temple in 1843. Temple registered his own brand in 1852 (*right*). *Rancho Los Cerritos Collection.*

the Nieto cattle brand. Temple paid each of Manuela's eleven heirs $272.75. Guillermo Cota, Manuela's husband and the executor of her will, signed the papers on behalf of his younger children who were not yet of legal age. Her son Leonardo Cota signed deeds on behalf of his unmarried sisters and his brother Raymundo, who were not literate themselves. Illiterate married daughters' husbands signed on their behalf.

CHAPTER 3

CATTLE RANCHING IN THE MEXICAN ERA

After Mexico won its independence from Spanish rule in 1821, one of the major impacts in Alta California was the opening of the former colony to commerce with foreign traders. Although illicit trade had gone on during the colonial period, the ports of Monterey, San Pedro, Santa Barbara and San Diego were now officially open to vessels from the United States, South America and Europe, and foreigners began to arrive and settle in California. Many married Californianas, women of local Californio families, and formed part of Californio society. The future owner of Rancho Los Cerritos was one of these early foreign residents.

John Temple

John Temple (1796–1866) was born in Reading, Massachusetts, in 1796 to a prominent Congregationalist family. The Temples were descended from English Puritan immigrants who arrived in New England in 1636. Temple's father served as a captain in the local militia. As a young man, Temple began trading in the Sandwich Isles (today known as Hawai'i), later purchasing his own schooner.[103] Trade with the Sandwich Isles had opened up during the late 1700s with the arrival of foreign merchants and Protestant missionaries, and trade between Hawai'i and California, on ships that included large crews of *kanaka* (Hawaiian) sailors, was common. In a triangular trade route, merchant ships plying the coast of California traded hides and tallow for manufactured goods and carried the hides from California and sandalwood from Hawai'i back to New England.

Temple arrived in Monterey, California, in 1827 on the ship *Waverly* with his close friend William Dana and began to explore business possibilities in the ports of California. Historian and museum director Paul Spitzzeri cites a letter from Temple to a sea captain at this time in which Temple laconically described his life-altering decision: "I expect we shall sail for California in the course [of] six weeks."[104]

After deciding to stay and seek his fortune in California, Temple became a Mexican citizen and converted to Catholicism. Under Mexican law, citizens and naturalized citizens could acquire land; naturalized citizens were Catholic foreigners who swore to uphold the laws of Mexico.[105] He was baptized with the name Juan Bautista (for John the Baptist) at Mission San Diego and was known afterward as Don Juan. The term *Don*, used with a person's first name, was a mark of respect. As a Mexican citizen and Catholic, Temple would be able to marry and purchase land in Mexico more easily than a Protestant could. Interestingly, he applied for a *diligencia matrimonial*, a permit to marry, before he even met his intended bride.

One year after arriving in California, Temple opened a store in the Pueblo de Los Ángeles, the first mercantile store in the pueblo, near the *placita* or central square. Prior to the establishment of mercantile stores such as Temple's, people had to wait for the ships to come in to purchase or trade goods. Ships had to anchor offshore—three miles out, in the case of the port at San Pedro—and bring in goods and passengers on small craft called lighters.

Temple, on record as the second American or European resident of Los Angeles, had an adobe home near the intersection of what are today Main and Spring Streets.[106] On a trip north to Santa Barbara, he met his future wife, María Rafaela Benedicta Cota. It is possible that they met at the wedding of Temple's friend William Dana and Rafaela's friend Josefa Carrillo at the mission church in Santa Barbara. One family story, however, is that Temple courted Rafaela's sister before he courted her.[107]

Intermarriages between Californianas and foreigners became common during the Mexican period. From 1831 to 1839, sixty-eight marriages took place at the Santa Barbara Presidio; John and Rafaela's was one of the ten that involved foreigners.[108] Three of Rafaela's sisters also married foreigners. María Clara married the Italian José Lobero, Juana Lugarda married the Ecuadorian José Ramón Malo and María Altagracia married the American

John Temple circa 1860. *Rancho Los Cerritos Collection.*

Augustus Hinchman. Don Abel Stearns, Temple's neighbor and owner of Rancho Los Alamitos, married Arcadia Bandini. Fourteen-year-old Doña Arcadia, of the San Diego Bandini family, was known for her beauty. It was not unusual for a ranchero to select a wife much younger than himself. In the Temples' case, John was thirty-four and Rafaela was eighteen when they married. In the Stearns's case, however, the age difference between Don Abel, aged forty-three, and Doña Arcadia was notable.

Californio families tended to be large and were connected by elaborate networks of blood and fictive kinship, or *compadrazgo. Compadrazgo* refers to the bonds created through the selection of godparents for weddings and baptisms. In Hispanic society, the relationship between children's godparents and their actual parents is that of *compadres*, literally "co-parents." This relationship is as strong as that between godparents and their godchildren. Godparents (*padrinos* and *madrinas*) were selected from among family members, friends and associates and rancho owners. In Alta California, marriage into leading Californio families provided an advantage to foreign businessmen and traders like John Temple through access to these social networks. For Californio families, additional kinship ties with American and European traders "seemed to assure mutuality in trade and a degree of continuity with familiar traditions."[109]

Rafaela Cota de Temple

When Temple married Rafaela Cota (1812–1887), he married into a leading military family of Santa Barbara. The Cota family as well as the other families of soldiers and settlers from colonial Mexico were gente de razón.

Like most of the other elite families of early California, the Cota family claimed arrival in California on the Sacred Expedition of Portolá in 1769. Rafaela's great-grandfather Andrés Cota had arrived in California with Portolá, and her grandfather Pablo Antonio Cota arrived shortly thereafter. He was a member of the original Santa Barbara Presidio company, established in 1782, and was appointed *alferez* (second lieutenant) of the presidio in 1788. Rafaela's father was a soldado de cuera in the same company. Rafaela, the eldest of twelve children of Francisco Cota and María de Jesús Olivera, was born in 1812 at the presidio of Santa Barbara.

Presidios were typically laid out as a quadrangle around a *plaza de armas*, or central square where the troops assembled. In addition to offices, reception rooms and the chapel, rooms along the quadrangle included barracks for single soldiers and rooms for officers and soldiers with families. Married soldiers were allotted two-room residences within the presidio itself, with a small garden in the rear.[110] Some married soldiers occupied homes just outside of the presidio quadrangle.[111]

Although opportunities for schooling were very limited in Alta California, several women related in *testimonios*, or narratives, that they had been taught to read as girls in schools in their homes. The testimonios were collected in the latter part of the nineteenth century as part of historian George

Opposite: Rafaela Cota de Temple circa 1850. *Rancho Los Cerritos Collection.*

Above: Drawing depicting the living quarters for married soldiers at the Santa Barbara Presidio. *Courtesy of Santa Barabara Trust for Historic Preservation.*

Mission Santa Barbara. *Courtesy of Gledhill Library, Santa Barbara Historical Museum.*

Bancroft's research for his multivolume *History of California*. It is possible that Rafaela learned to read in a similar fashion.

Life in the frontier outpost of Alta California was precarious, and settlers lived under the ongoing prospect of uprisings by Indigenous people who resisted conquest and assimilation. Indigenous rebellions against the missions, with threats to kill the gente de razón families living in settlements surrounding the missions, were a constant, looming possibility. One such attack occurred at the missions of Santa Barbara, Santa Inés and La Purísima when Rafaela was eleven years old. Indians drove settlers from their homes around Mission Santa Barbara and fought off soldiers from the presidio for several hours. The mission was looted before the Indians vanished into the surrounding hills. At nearby Santa Inés, the mission was burned, and at La Purísima the gente de razón families were seized but not killed. Troops went after the Indians, who had fled into the tulares.[112]

A Californio Wedding

Doña Rafaela Cota and Don Juan Temple were married at the church of Mission Santa Barbara in 1830. William Dana and Josefa Carrillo de Dana stood as witnesses to the occasion. It is possible that their wedding was similar to that of Doña Anita de la Guerra to Alfred Robinson, which also took place in the mission at Santa Barbara:

> *At ten o'clock the bride went up with her sister to the confessional, dressed in deep black. Nearly an hour intervened, when the great doors of the Mission church opened, the bells rang out a loud, discordant peal, the bride, dressed in complete white, came out of the church with the bridegroom, followed by a long procession.*[113]

Another Californio tradition that Don Juan may have followed was for the groom to remove his sash, use it to lift his new bride onto his horse and ride off with her. It is likely that Don Juan and Doña Rafaela were saluted with a fusillade because of her family's prominence in Santa Barbara society and their military roots. Californio weddings were often followed by several days of feasting, dancing and celebration. In her testimonio, Angustias de la Guerra recalled the custom of cracking *cascarones*, eggshells filled with confetti and perfume, on the heads of unsuspecting guests at these parties.[114]

Life in the Pueblo

After the wedding, Don Juan and eighteen-year-old Doña Rafaela settled in the pueblo of Los Angeles, in a two-story adobe home on Calle Principal, later known as Main Street. Their daughter Francisca was born one year later. She was christened Francisca Borja de Jesús Temple at the pueblo church. The pueblo, with a population of 770 gentes de razón and 198 Indigenous people in 1830, was a rough frontier town.[115] The houses were made of adobe, the great majority of them being single-story buildings. The claylike streets turned into streams of mud after rainstorms. Murder was common; a death a day was not unusual.[116]

Citizens responded to what they perceived as lawless circumstances in the pueblo by taking matters into their own hands. The first Vigilance Committee, made up of fifty-five prominent citizens, was formed in 1836 after the murder of ranchero Domingo Féliz by his wife, María Villa, and her lover Gervasio Alipas. The committee, which included Temple as well as Rafaela's second cousin Guillermo Cota, met in Temple's store and signed a petition demanding the culprits' execution. When the municipal council refused to act, the vigilante mob shot and killed María and her lover for the murder.[117] Governor Chico was incensed by the actions of the vigilante mob and threatened to arrest all fifty-five signers of the petition. He later pardoned all but a handful, realizing that they constituted the elite of the pueblo.

In addition to operating his store in the pueblo and participating in vigilante actions, Temple traded up and down the coast. One of his business partners was Thomas Larkin in Monterey. Temple's letters reveal his indignation with Larkin in 1839 (and possibly his own cantankerous nature) over a deal in which Larkin traded flour for Temple's *aguardiente* (brandy). Temple complained about finding himself in possession of flour for which there was not a market and rejected Larkin's offer of fifty dollars a barrel for twenty-seven barrels of aguardiente after they had agreed on sixty. Larkin's reply indicated his frustration with the deal.

> *You need not* repeat, *that you have my signature for payment of $60 Etc. I also know you have. I thought that you would be willing to take good flour at a fair price, in order to continue trade between us. It seams* [sic] *not!*[118]

Larkin and Temple continued to do business, complaints notwithstanding, and Temple's business ventures prospered. Temple's younger half-brother, nineteen-year-old Pliny Fisk Temple, arrived in 1841 and sought employment in his brother's store. In 1845, Jonathan and colleague David Alexander purchased from Abel Stearns the Casa de San Pedro, a store and warehouse in San Pedro from which they sold hides and tallow to incoming ships.[119]

After the birth of Francisca, Doña Rafaela often traveled north with her daughter to visit her family. Her father had been appointed administrator of Mission Santa Inés, north of Santa Barbara, and she made trips there. She is listed as godmother, or madrina, to several children, including Indigenous children at the mission. In one of his letters to family in Massachusetts, Pliny described his brother's wife as "a short, thick-set woman with fair complexion, the daughter Francisca is a fine little girl. I wish she was where she could be learning something, as there is no school here."[120]

At her home in Los Angeles, Rafaela supervised Indigenous servants who carried out the work of food preparation, cleaning, laundry, tending the home garden and collecting firewood. Native workers made up the workforce of the pueblo and were consigned to live in segregated plots of land, relocated several times, on the outskirts of the pueblo.[121] Rafaela's servants may have been among those receiving one dollar a day; however, most servants received less.[122]

Temple family tradition, as recounted by one of Pliny's descendants at a ceremony at Rancho Los Cerritos in 1969, has it that Doña Rafaela played a key role in supporting the romance between Pliny and his future bride, Antonia Margarita Workman. As Thomas Workman Temple II stated:

> *In the fall of 1842, just a year after the arrival of the Workman-Rowland party at the Pueblo de Los Angeles from Santa Fe, New Mexico, Julian Workman of Rancho La Puente brought his wife and daughter into the Pueblo to do some shopping. They made for Don Juan Temple's store, whose shelves were known to be laden with tempting wares from the Orient and the latest dimity and calicos from far off Boston and Salem. A short, blond clerk waited upon the ladies in broken Spanish. Don Juan and his wife, Doña Rafaela, who happened by chance to be downstairs, introduced the shy young Yankee behind the counter as Don Juan's youngest brother, Pliny. This was a fateful meeting for Antonia Margarita and Pliny, for it proved to be love at first sight. On successive visits to the Pueblo and Temple's store, the* señorita *lost her heart to the reserved Yankee clerk.*[123]

Doña Rafaela undoubtedly enjoyed Christmas customs with her family. As recounted by early California resident Don Arturo Bandini, the people of the pueblo of Los Angeles climbed to the roofs of their adobe homes to view the procession of rancheros from the surrounding ranchos coming to town for Christmas mass. Their families rode on horseback or in wooden oxcarts festooned with silken bedspreads, embroidered *rebosos* (shawls) and lace curtains.

A high point of the Christmas festivities was the performing of the traditional *pastorela* play in the courtyards of some of the larger adobe homes. The pastorela play, dating from medieval times and brought to the colonies from Spain, recounts the trek of the shepherds on their way to Bethlehem to see the Christ child. The climax of this lively rendition of the Christmas story is a sword fight between good and evil in the form of the Devil and the angel St. Michael. Bandini contended that the old American settlers, most of whom were from the state of Massachusetts, "fell heart and soul in with these customs, enjoying and encouraging all kinds of performances with a zeal and ardor equal to that of the native Californians."[124] It is quite possible that John Temple, who styled himself Don Juan in Californio fashion, was one of them.

Purchase of the Rancho

At about this time, Temple was contemplating expanding his interests into ranching and the hide and tallow business. He had the opportunity to accompany his friend Don Abel Stearns when he looked at the Rancho Los Alamitos property. Rancho Los Alamitos was one of the five ranchos that had previously formed part of the large Los Nietos land grant along with Rancho Los Cerritos. That trip probably piqued Temple's interest, and shortly thereafter he purchased Los Cerritos from the heirs of Manuela Nieto de Cota for $3,000. He paid half in gold and half in goods from his store in the pueblo and paid an additional $25 for the old Nieto brand.

Although the Cota adobe was located on the rancho, Temple envisioned a more elaborate home for his family. The house near the Los Angeles River that he would later refer to as his "jewel on a hill" served as the center of his cattle business and a summer residence for the family. Indigenous laborers made the sun-dried adobe bricks that were used to build the structure. The house, one of the first multilevel buildings in Southern California, was laid out in a U shape around a central *patio*, or courtyard. Single-story wings housed workrooms, workers' sleeping quarters and storerooms, while the two-story center section held the family residence.

The house was constructed in what came to be called Monterey colonial style, which developed in California during the Mexican period and merged elements from New England construction with adobe homes. Constructed in 1837, the Monterey home of Thomas Larkin—Temple's business partner and, later, American consul in Alta California during the Mexican-American War—is cited as the first example of this style and probably influenced Temple's design. The style features thick adobe walls, wooden floors, interior staircases and a second-story veranda. From the low hill on which the Cerritos adobe home was built, the willow-lined Los Angeles River could be seen. A visitor to the property in 1856 described Temple's rancho as "a beautiful region of country, extending to the ocean.…[It] commands a fine view of the country for more than 50 miles."[125]

Drawing of Rancho Los Cerritos in the 1850s. *Rancho Los Cerritos Collection.*

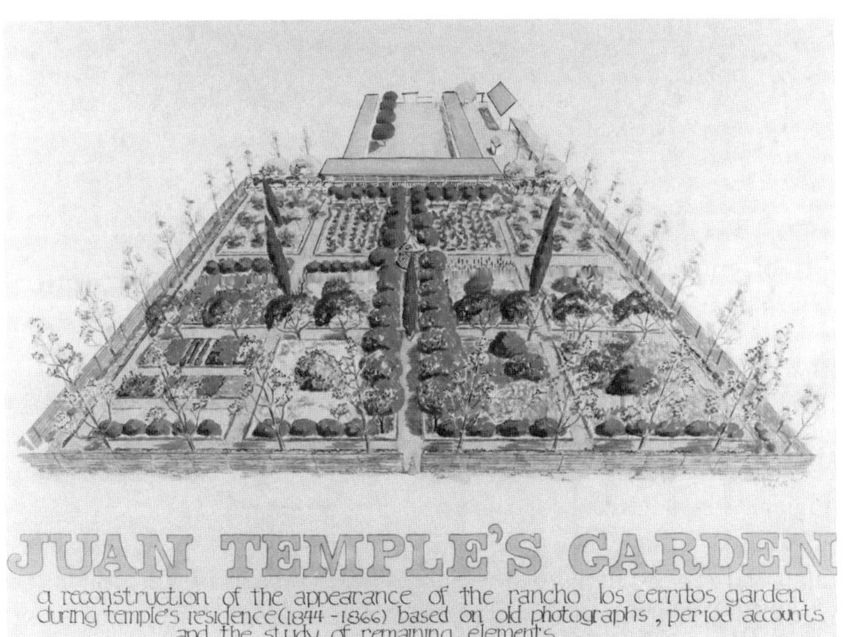

Drawing of John Temple's formal garden. *Rancho Los Cerritos Collection.*

Daguerreotype of John Temple and Rafaela with their son-in-law Gregorio de Ajuria, circa 1850s. *Rancho Los Cerritos Collection.*

Temple dedicated particular attention to the creation of a two-acre garden behind the adobe, surrounded by a redwood fence. Inspired by the formal gardens of his New England homeland, he requested that his brother Abraham send seeds for peach, plum, cherry, chestnut and black locust trees. He obtained cuttings from the San Gabriel mission for citrus and olive trees, grapes and roses. The garden was irrigated by means of a hydraulic ram that pumped water from the river to a cistern. In 1848, Don Juan and Doña Rafaela's daughter Francisca married the Spaniard Gregorio de Ajuria, and the couple honeymooned at the recently completed Rancho home.

José Roco, Leno, Teresa and Tupajuria

After purchasing the Rancho, Don Juan increased its herds, running up to fifteen thousand head of cattle, seven thousand sheep and three thousand horses on the land. The Temple family had their main residence in the pueblo of Los Angeles and stayed at the Rancho during summers and rodeos and for entertaining. The census of 1850 lists the workers and their families who actually resided at the Rancho on a permanent basis. At most ranchos, and probably at Los Cerritos as well, workers were provided food and rudimentary living quarters in *jacales* (shacks) and were paid in kind, sometimes with aguardiente, a local brandy, or finished goods such as blankets or clothing.[126]

The 1850 census not only documents a diverse workforce but also includes information about the residents' birthplace, age and Indian or non-Indian status. The *mayordomo*, or ranch manager, was listed as José Roco, an unmarried Spaniard age thirty-three. Since Don Juan did not reside permanently at the Rancho, the role of the mayordomo in supervising staff and workers and keeping accounts was key.

The majority of the workers at Rancho Los Cerritos were Indigenous people, as was true of ranchos throughout the state. Most workers were Tongva, along with people of other tribes such as the Cahuila and Serrano that had been brought together at Mission San Gabriel. With the secularization of the missions, mission Indians had been put off their land and went either to ranchos or pueblos in search of work.[127] Seasonal workers were added at the peak work periods of roundups and slaughter of cattle.

The census lists all male workers at Rancho Los Cerritos other than the mayordomo as laborers, without designating the type of work done. Some were vaqueros, or cowboys, but other workers likely included those with skills in carpentry and blacksmithing. A common rancho worker was a *mandadero*, or servant, who did odd jobs such as chopping wood, carrying water and sweeping the yard.[128] Of the male workers, one other besides José Roco was from Spain, one was from the Sandwich Isles and six were Californios.

As was also typical of social norms of the time, the Indigenous people recorded are listed by their first name only. Leno, age thirty, was one of these Indigenous workers, very likely a vaquero. Vaqueros were the cowboys who worked directly with the herds of cattle. They were superb horsemen and extremely skillful in the use of the *reata*, or lasso. Vaqueros were responsible

51

SCHEDULE I.—Free Inhabitants in ______ **in the County of** Los Angeles **State of** California **enumerated by me, on the** 6th **day of** Feby **1850.** [illegible] **Ass't Marshal.** 26

	Dwelling-houses numbered in the order of visitation.	Families numbered in the order of visitation.	The Name of every Person whose usual place of abode on the first day of June, 1850, was in this family.	Description: Age.	Sex.	Color, White, black, or mulatto.	Profession, Occupation, or Trade of each Male Person over 15 years of age.	Value of Real Estate owned.	Place of Birth. Naming the State, Territory, or Country.	Married within the year.	Attended School within the year.	Persons over 20 y'rs of age who cannot read & write.	Whether deaf and dumb, blind, insane, idiotic, pauper, or convict.	
	1	2	3	4	5	6	7	8	9	10	11	12	13	
1			Thomas Head	25	M		Laborer		Mo					1
2			James Carpenter	25	M		Laborer		Mo					2
3			William Sanford	30	M		Laborer		Mo					3
4			Thomas Morgan	30	M		Laborer		Ireland					4
5			Thomas S Hanford	21	M		None		Ar					5
6			Baltazar	35	M		Laborer		Mex			/		6
7			Thomas Taglisle	23	M		Laborer		England			/		7
8			Robert Tarbrook	15	M		Laborer		England					8
9			George H Burton	23	M		CH Officer		N Y					9
10	321	321	Jose Simon Roco	33	M		Manager		Spain					10
11			Juan M Olivera	38	M		Laborer		Ca			/		11
12			Dolores Olivera	18	f				Ca					12
13			Manuel J Fojo	45	M		Laborer		Spain			/		13
14			Nicolasa Fojo	40	f				Ca			/		14
15			Casimiro Lara	30	M		Laborer		Ca					15
16			Rafael Lisalda	21	M		Laborer		Ca			/		16
17			Rafael Ruiz	23	M		Laborer		Ca			/		17
18			Francis	16	f				Ca					18
19			Felipe Ruedo	28	M		Laborer		Ca			/		19
20			Vicenta	27	f				Ca			/		20
21			Francisca	2	f				Ca					21
22			Tupajuria	35	M		Laborer		Sanmiguel			/		22
23			Alen	40	M	I	Laborer		Ca			/		23
24			Maria	16	f	I			Ca					24
25			Sisto	30	M	I	Laborer		Ca			/		25
26			Lucas	52	M	I	Laborer		Ca			/		26
27			Gina	30	f	I			Ca			/		27
28			Salome	18	f	I			Ca					28
29			Diega	10	f	I			Ca					29
30			Merced	8	f	I			Ca					30
31			Ventura	12	f	I			Ca					31
32			Julian Padilla	55	M		Laborer		Ca			/		32
33			Jose Maria	1	M	I			Ca					33
34			Manuel	7	M	I			Ca					34
35			Georga	25	f	I			Ca			/		35
36			Marta	3	f	I			Ca					36
37			Lino	30	M	I	Laborer		Ca			/		37
38			Teresa	20	f	I			Ca			/		38
39			Ramon	2	M	I			Ca					39
40			Josefa	1	f	I			Ca					40
41			Manuel	30	M	I	Laborer		Ca			/		41
42			Venancio	22	M	I	Laborer		Ca			/		42

An 1850 census page showing residents of Rancho Los Cerritos. *Public domain.*

for both branding the young calves and slaughtering the mature cows. A visitor to Rancho Cucamonga wrote in his diary, "I have seen some very good riders in Mexico, but these Californians are much better, and it is said they will throw the lasso better with their feet than Mexicans can with the hand."[129] The names following Leno's on the 1850 census are most likely those of his family: his wife, Teresa, age twenty, and their children, two-year-old Ramón and one-year-old Josefa.

Although women undoubtedly worked in their own households as well as the main house, their work was not recorded in the census. Leno's wife, Teresa, worked grinding corn and cooking, sewing and doing laundry as well as caring for her two small children. The older children of rancho families helped with tasks alongside their elders or were apprenticed to learn specialized work such as that of the vaqueros. A later vaquero, Miguel Murillo, remembered learning to break horses at Rancho Los Cerritos at age fourteen.

Tupajuria is listed as a laborer, age thirty-five, from the Sandwich Isles, today the Hawaiian Islands. *Kanaka*, or Hawaiians, had been coming to California on merchant ships and whaling vessels since the 1820s, and some stayed on to become part of California society. Some, like Tupajuria, learned the skills of caring for cattle and worked on ranchos as vaqueros.

Mission-trained Indigenous vaqueros also played a role in the growth of the cattle industry in the Hawaiian Islands themselves. In his voyages of exploration, Captain George Vancouver brought cattle to Hawai'i in the late 1700s, where the herds quickly multiplied, causing damage to gardens and sugarcane patches and even endangering people's lives. King Kamehameha III sent a royal decree to mission contacts in California, requesting that experienced vaqueros come to Hawai'i to teach Hawaiians the basics of roping and herding. In 1830, a group of about a dozen Indigenous vaqueros—three each for the four major islands—arrived with their trained mustangs and specialized gear to instruct the local population in herd management. Eleven years later, a Hawaiian newspaper reported that these original vaqueros were no longer needed; they had been replaced by the Hawaiian *paniolo*, or cowboys. The term *paniolo* is most likely a rendering in the Hawaiian language of *español*.[130] Thus the Hawaiian cattle industry at large ranches such as the Parker Ranch in Waimea on the island of Hawai'i began with California vaquero support.

Rancho Work and the Hide and Tallow Trade

Since the establishment of the missions, cattle had been raised for their hides and tallow, or fat, which was rendered for the production of soap and candles. After secularization of the missions, privately owned ranchos carried on the hide and tallow trade. Cattle ranges were not fenced, so the cattle roamed freely and mingled with those of other ranchos. Ownership was determined by their brand, a permanent and distinct scar marked on the steer's hip.

One aspect of the annual roundups of cattle that characterized the California experience was the "run through the mustard," when vaqueros were forced to drive cattle through mustard-covered hillsides. The mustard plant is an invasive species unknown in California prior to conquest. A common explanation is that it was brought by the mission friars. The mustard plants seen today on California hillsides are low plants. In rancho days, however, the mustard plants were described as growing to six feet tall and, at times, taller than a man on horseback. Cattle among the mustard plants on the open hillsides were not visible and thus needed to be flushed out by horsemen on a "run through the mustard."

Mexican law required each ranchero to hold a general roundup, or rodeo, each year in the springtime to brand the new calves (before they were weaned). All neighboring rancheros were notified of the event, and an established code of conduct governed these rodeos. Overseen by a designated government official, a *juez del campo* ("judge of the plain"), the vaqueros from all the nearby ranches rounded up the cattle and branded any unbranded animals. The juez del campo arranged for the rodeo and held an informal court, on horseback or on the open hillside, to settle disputes that arose during the roundup. Ownership of each calf was determined by the brand on the calf's mother, and the host ranchero usually received those whose lineage was uncertain. Cattle that had strayed from a neighbor's herd were properly marked and returned.[131] Don Juan Temple himself was known to have served as a juez del campo on at least one occasion, according to an 1854 article in the *Star*.[132]

Many of the customs associated with cattle ranching—such as the figure of the juez del campo, the rules that governed registration of brands, the carrying out of the rodeo and the equipment used by the vaqueros themselves—were developed over time on the ranches of Spain. This knowledge was brought to the New World, first to central Mexico and from there to the territory of Alta California. Equipment such as the braided rawhide rope (*reata*, which became *lariat* in English) and the leather coverings to protect the legs was fashioned by the vaquero himself following these traditions. The modern cowboy of today owes his origin to California's vaqueros, who were working cattle nearly eighty years before the first "American" cowboys.

These yearly rodeos, or roundups of cattle from open ranges, were big events, and all the ranchos participated. Horace Bell described a rodeo at Rancho San Joaquín in 1853 at which more than one hundred vaqueros worked:

> *The Machados of La Ballona, the Picos from San Fernando and San Diego, the Dominguez, the Sepulvedas of Palos Verdes, the Lugos from everywhere, the Avilas of Tahauta, Centinela, and Aliso, the Sanchez, the Ocampo, and the Cotas, the Stearns, Rowlands, Reeds, Williams, the Yorbas of Santa Ana, and the Temples of Puente and Cerritos, all were there.*[133]

The roundups were followed by *fiestas*, or parties, lasting several days. During the day, vaqueros competed in horse racing or in contests such as the rooster pull, in which a rider would lean down from his galloping horse and try to grab a rooster that was buried to its neck in sand. Bear fighting was another popular activity. In this brutal and uniquely Californian spectacle, one of a bear's paws was tied to the foreleg of a bull, and the two fought in an enclosed corral until one was killed.[134] In the evenings, there was dancing, music and feasting on roasted meat. In her testimonio, María Antonia Rodríguez recalled what she described as the national dance of the Californios:

> *The jarabe is a dance that is quite similar to the jig that is all the rage with the Americans from the states of Virginia and Alabama. Only two people dance the jarabe. The dancers would stand facing each other, and at the sound of a harp, a vihuela, and a violin, they would move their legs in such a way that it was a pleasure to watch them. It was customary to reward the best female dancer with a prize. This is how the prize was given: some of the people in attendance would take off their hats and put them on the female dancer's head.*[135]

A similar *jarabe*, the *jarabe tapatío* or *jarabe* of Guadalajara, is today considered the national dance of Mexico.

Another part of ranch life was the yearly *matanza*, or slaughter of mature cattle for their hides and tallow. After being separated from the meat and

A fandango, or party with dancing and music, during the Mexican period. *Courtesy of New York Public Library.*

tallow, the hides were cured by soaking them in large pots of salt water (brine). Then they were dried by laying them in the hot sun and holding them down with pegs. Once dry, the hides were hard and stiff. Ranch workers sometimes tanned hides domestically and used the rawhide to braid reatas, resole boots and make window shades. However, most of the hides were shipped around Cape Horn at the southernmost tip of South America to factories on the East Coast of the United States for further processing into leather goods like boots and saddles.

The cattle hides were sometimes referred to as California banknotes and had a value of about two dollars each. It was true that leading California rancheros were wealthy in terms of land and cattle, including California banknotes, but they often had little in the way of actual money. John Temple, however, due to his primary occupation as trader and businessman, had more money than most other Southern California landowners.

Workers took the best cuts of meat for cooking or drying to make beef jerky; however, because of the small population of the territory, demand for meat was limited and most was not used. After the matanza, the carcasses were left in the fields to rot.[136] During the Mexican period, it was common for travelers passing through rancho lands to be granted permission to slaughter a steer as needed for food, but they were requested to leave the hide staked for the ranchero to claim.[137]

The tallow (or cow fat) was rendered in large trypots (*try* means to render or clarify by melting). The rendered tallow was then poured into *botas*, or rawhide bags. The best tallow was used in cooking and making soap and candles. Tallow candles tend to be smoky and not particularly sweet-scented, so the elite families who could afford the expense, such as the Cotas and Temples, used paraffin candles. Tallow candles were used in workshops and were shipped to Mexico and South America for use in the mines. The tallow from one cow would be sold for another two dollars. The hides and tallow were transported by *carretas*, or ox-pulled carts, to the port of San Pedro for purchase by trading ships.

Stratified Rancho Life

A famous horse race of the period took place between horses from Rancho Los Cerritos and Rancho Los Alamitos. The Alamitos, one of the five ranchos resulting from the division of Rancho Los Nietos, was owned by Yankee immigrant and merchant Don Abel Stearns. The race began on Signal Hill, known as El Cerro at the time, and went down to the sea (following the path of what is today Alamitos Avenue in Long Beach), around a stake and back to the starting point.[138] Temple's horse, El Beserero, won him the prize of one thousand head of cattle.

Social conditions were such that the owner of a rancho could afford to bet one thousand head of cattle on a single horse race and could provide days of feasting for hundreds of neighbors, their families and their workers. Rancho wealth was produced, however, by a largely Indigenous workforce that received minimal compensation for their labor and few options for betterment. Conditions varied from rancho to rancho. In some cases, skilled vaqueros were able to command wages of one dollar a day (equivalent to roughly forty dollars today); in others, workers received compensation in aguardiente and goods rather than cash.[139]

At some ranchos, workers were able to leave to seek better conditions—such as one of the workers at Rancho Los Cerritos, an Indian named Querino, who fled an impending flogging at Los Cerritos to seek work at Rancho Los Alamitos. Conditions at other ranchos were described by observers as peonage, in which workers were bound to the land through debt.

Rancho workers could be hired annually or seasonally. After American occupation of California, seasonal or occasional workers could be purchased in weekly auctions in the pueblo of Los Angeles. The administrator of Rancho Los Alamitos reported doing so, and occasional workers were most likely acquired in this manner at Los Cerritos as well. Ordinances passed in the pueblo required the arrest and fining of Indians found guilty of public drunkenness. Those unable to pay their fine were subject to auction to employers who paid the fine in exchange for one week's work, at the end of which the worker was paid in part in aguardiente, leading to a weekly cycle of alcohol abuse and unpaid labor. Horace Bell described the system: "Los Angeles has its slave mart as well as New Orleans and Constantinople—only the slave at Los Angeles was sold fifty-two times a year as long as he lives."[140]

Cultural Perspectives

Foreigners who visited or came to reside in Alta California often recorded their impressions of Californio society and customs. Their books, diaries and letters provide interesting firsthand details of life in California during the Mexican era. Their writings include the prejudices of the day and assumptions of Protestant Anglo-Saxon superiority. Perhaps the most widely cited is Richard Henry Dana's influential *Two Years Before the Mast.* Amid descriptions of his adventures at sea, Dana shared his impressions of the people he met in port. He decried the treatment of the Indigenous people—"Of the poor Indians, very little care is taken"—and he was unstinting in his critique of the Californios, whom he described as thriftless, proud and extravagant. The Californianas were described as having "a great deal of beauty, and their morality, of course, is none the best."[141]

The casual "of course" in Dana's remark is telling. In his assumptions about the women's immoral behavior, Dana echoes elements of the anti-Spanish propaganda that has been called the Black Legend, perpetuated in Protestant Europe for several centuries.[142] From the time of the reign of Queen Elizabeth I, English pamphleteers had characterized (caricatured) Spaniards as immoral, the spawn of Satan, evil and cruel. Spain's rule of its American colonies was painted as uniquely authoritarian, backward, medieval, arbitrary and ineffective in comparison with that of Protestant colonizers. These implicit beliefs influenced how Protestant Anglo Americans approached, understood and judged Californio society.

Dana was not alone in his judgments of the Californios. Others described idle rancheros spending their days on horseback riding aimlessly across the hills. When Anita de la Guerra's husband, Alfred Robinson, anonymously published his book *Travels in California*, her brother, Senator Pablo de la Guerra, considered the book quite biased. Anita contended that the people involved in the incidents described would not even recognize themselves in the narrative.[143]

Deeply held assumptions of Protestant Anglo cultural and racial superiority formed the foundation of the concept of Manifest Destiny: the belief that the United States was destined to extend its rule—with its republican form of government, Protestant religion and American way of life—from the East Coast to the West.[144] A term first used in an editorial in a New York City newspaper, *manifest destiny* formed the basis of the 1844 presidential platform of Democratic candidate James Polk. Bolstered by the assumptions of manifest destiny, the United States looked to the south, to war with Mexico, as the means of attaining its destiny. Historian Mario Barrera characterizes manifest destiny as a "manipulated appeal and attempt to secure broad popular support for an expansionist policy of particular benefit to certain political and economic interests."[145] Assumptions of racial superiority fostered the belief among squatters who had taken up residence illegally on rancho lands owned by others that these lands were not being used effectively and could be put to better purpose by thrifty and energetic American settlers. When war between Mexico and the United States eventually broke out, Rancho Los Cerritos played a role in the struggle.

CHAPTER 4

MEXICAN-AMERICAN WAR, STATEHOOD AND TRANSITION FOR THE RANCHO

The years leading up to the war between Mexico and the United States had been marked by political divisions and unrest in Mexican California. During the twenty-five years of Mexican rule (1821–1846), Alta California saw fifteen governors (if one counts the periods when different governors claimed dominion over the northern and southern regions of the territory). There were twelve rebellions during this period, when Californios sought to dislodge a governor, defy a governor or ensure that their favorite occupied the governor's post.[146] At times Californios, aided increasingly by foreign residents, united to expel unpopular governors. At other times factions battled for internal control.

Mexican California on the Verge of War

In 1842, Manuel Micheltorena was appointed governor of Alta California by the centrist Mexican government. His rule was opposed by Californios, who had become accustomed to having a voice in choosing their own administrators under the federalist constitution of 1824. Chief among those opposing Micheltorena in the south was Pío Pico. Pico entrusted the foreign contingent of his armed rebel forces to William Workman, Pliny Temple's father-in-law. Pico later related that he counted among his supporters William Workman and John Temple. Micheltorena eventually surrendered authority to Pío Pico and left Alta California, but not before advising Pico that war between Mexico and the United States was imminent.[147]

President Polk, elected in 1844 after a campaign dominated by the theme of western expansion of the United States, sought to provoke war with Mexico. Before formal hostilities were declared, he sent Captain John Frémont of the Army Corps of Topographical Engineers on a mission to California with discretion to act as events presented themselves. Californio leaders, meanwhile, were at odds about how to proceed. Governor Castro in the north advocated for seeking support from Britain or France to protect California from hordes of Yankee immigrants. Don Mariano Vallejo, a leading landowner in the north, supported the idea of seeking annexation to the United States, in what would be a similar move to that enacted in Texas the previous decade.

At the same time that Polk was provoking war with Mexico by marching troops into a border region in Texas between the Rio Grande and the Nueces River that was considered by Mexico to be its northern border, Frémont moved to provoke an uprising by American settlers in the Sacramento River area of northern California in what became known as the Bear Flag Revolt. Armed American settlers, most of whom had resided in California for only a year or two, marched into the town of Sonoma and arrested Mariano Vallejo and his brother, brother-in-law and secretary, among other leading Californios. The captives were held at Sutter's Fort while American consul Thomas Larkin, who was on good terms with Californio leaders, attempted to persuade the Californios to voluntarily place their homeland under U.S. control. Pío Pico, in control of Californio troops in the south, however, declared that the illegal Bear Flag rebellion and the incarceration of the Vallejos made capitulation impossible.[148]

In the aftermath of the Bear Flag Revolt, Abel Stearns served as sub-prefect with Pío Pico's forces in the south. At a meeting in Stearns's Los Angeles home, a group of citizens denounced General Castro, whom they believed (unjustly, as it turned out) was using the opportunity of opposition to American takeover to stage a coup of his own. The resolution denouncing Castro was signed by the eighty citizens attending the meeting, twenty-five of whom were Americans, including John Temple.

Don Juan and Doña Rafaela During the Mexican-American War

Americans and Europeans who had made their homes in early California participated socially, economically and politically in Californio society. Referred to with the honorific "Don," many owed their fortunes to connections and opportunities made possible in Californio society. It was not always clear where foreigners' loyalties lay, however, when it came to war between the United States and Mexico. Americans in California undoubtedly experienced discomfort as their native country entered into hostilities with the land in which they had raised their families, achieved economic success and established ties of kinship and compadrazgo with local Californios.

In the spring of 1846, the American army marched from New Mexico and into San Diego in Southern California, while American naval forces seized Monterey in the north. With the intent of taking the pueblo of Los Angeles, Frémont led land forces up from San Diego, and Commodore Stockton arrived at the port of San Pedro by ship. When the American leaders heard that a large number of Californios were at Abel Stearns's Rancho Los Alamitos, they decided to meet at Temple's Rancho Los Cerritos. From there, the American forces marched unimpeded into the pueblo and established martial law. Stockton named John Temple alcalde, or mayor, of the pueblo and left a garrison of fifty soldiers under the command of Marine Lieutenant Archibald Gillespie.[149]

Gillespie imposed unnecessarily austere restrictions on the local population, including the imposition of a curfew, search and seizure of goods in private homes and limitations on citizens' freedom of association.[150] These conditions sparked rebellion by the local citizens, who attacked the garrison. As the situation worsened, Gillespie sent a messenger, a young Swede known locally as Juan Flaco ("Thin John"), to ride north from the city to request reinforcements from Commodore Stockton. Flaco waited for Temple, as mayor, to give the password to the guard so he could leave. Temple instead shouted out, "Don't shoot the man on the white horse!" His shout was overheard by a group of Californios, who rode off in pursuit of Flaco. Although they succeeded in shooting his horse, Flaco made his escape. Gillespie was forced to surrender before reinforcements appeared, however, and he and his forces left by ship from San Pedro.

Temple's motivations and allegiance are difficult to ascertain. Was he alerting the Californios to the messenger's task on purpose, or was he rather

Portraits of John Temple (*left*) and Rafaela Cota de Temple (*right*) by William S. Jewett, both 1856. *Rancho Los Cerritos Collection.*

clumsily exerting his authority as mayor? We know that Temple himself declined to stay in the pueblo, instead taking his family to their rancho residence for the remainder of the war. Californio Enrique Ávila recounted that Doña Rafaela took advantage of their flight to take ammunition from their store to donate to the Californio army.[151] An oft repeated, if unsubstantiated, version has it that she hid gunpowder under her skirts as she traveled out of the pueblo by oxcart. We have no record of how Doña Rafaela's activities might have been viewed by her husband or what she thought about his actions.

Doña Rafaela's actions in support of the Californio cause mirror other actions taken by Californianas and recounted in their testimonios. Angustias de la Guerra described to the Bancroft project interviewer how she hid a wounded Californio soldier from American troops who came searching for him at her home while her husband was away.[152] She was in bed, recovering from giving birth, and hid the soldier under the blankets with her, placing her baby on top. She described the American lieutenant entering her bedchamber with a candle in one hand and a pistol in the other. He held the pistol up to her face before admitting that the wounded soldier had not been found. Another Californiana, Rosalía Vallejo, stated bitterly that she refused to learn English because she wanted nothing to do with the Americans who had taken her husband prisoner during the Bear Flag Revolt.[153]

In October the same year, an American force led by Gillespie and reinforced by Captain Mervine's troops landed once again at San Pedro in an effort to retake Los Angeles. They met the Californio forces at the Domínguez rancho, not far from Rancho Los Cerritos, in what has since been referred to as the Battle of the Old Woman's Gun. The Californio horsemen, led by José Carrillo, were outnumbered and armed with lances, but they had obtained a four-pound cannon that had been hidden away by an old woman and her daughter in a tule patch near their home. Using their reatas, the Californios dragged the cannon in pursuit of the American troops as they retreated to San Pedro. The old woman who donated the cannon was fifty-seven-year-old María Clara Cota de Reyes, a relative of Rafaela's.

Following the Californio victory at the Domínguez rancho, the Californio leader José María Flores camped his regiment at the Cerritos rancho.[154] When Stockton arrived at the San Pedro harbor, Flores had his mounted troops drive a herd of horses back and forth within sight of the ship. The movement and dust thrown up by the horses convinced Stockton that Californio forces outnumbered his own, so he ordered the ship to return to San Diego without engaging in battle. Guillermo Cota's son, Francisco Cota, was a participant in the event.

Later, in November, Americans taken prisoner by Flores' troops at the Williams family adobe at Rancho del Chino were housed at Rancho Los Cerritos. It is not clear if Temple hosted the prisoners or if he, too, was being detained. In a letter to his brother in 1847, he complained of losses calculated at $10,000, stating, "I and brother Pliny have passed many anxious days and nights during the insurrection, our persons and families exposed to insult and imprisonment."[155]

Following the defeat of the last Californio army near Los Angeles, General Andrés Pico signed a surrender agreement at Cahuenga Pass on January 13, 1847. With the signing of the Treaty of Guadalupe Hidalgo in 1848, Mexico ceded to the United States 55 percent of its territory, which included the present states of California, Arizona, New Mexico, Nevada and Utah and parts of Colorado and Wyoming. Mexican negotiators did their utmost to protect the rights of Mexican citizens living in the areas that were now part of the United States; however, none of the articles in the treaty protected the rights of Indigenous people. Articles VIII and IX of the treaty gave assurances regarding the property and citizenship rights of the Mexicans in the newly conquered territories. Article VIII gave U.S. citizenship to all Mexicans who wanted it. Article IX promised that these people "in the meantime shall be maintained and protected in the free enjoyment of their liberty and property and secured in the free exercise of their religion without restriction." However, the final version of the treaty ratified by the U.S. Senate omitted Article X, which had contained stronger language protecting land rights, stating that grants of land made by the Mexican government would be respected as valid.[156] The deletion of this article would later prove disastrous for many Mexican landholders in California.

As she reflected on the impact of the U.S. takeover of Alta California, Angustias de la Guerra commented on the differences between the two cultures:

> *One time, when a Spaniard named Don Gregorio Ajuria was in my living room engaged in conversation, he had something in his pocket that appeared to be bothering him. He stuck his hand in his pocket and pulled out two pieces of gold. He gave them to my daughter Carolina to play with. Soon after, I went into the dining room and found my American friend Don Eduardo Ord weighing gold on a small scale. Every time he emptied the scale, he would clean it so that none of the precious gold dust would be left behind. When it was time to eat, I told the two of them and several other friends that I had seen an interesting contrast in the morning. On the one hand, we see a Spaniard throwing gold around because it is bothering him, and on the other hand we have a Yankee who cleans the plate on his scale with the same care that a priest cleans the paten.*[157]

Forty-Niners Rush In

The ending of the Mexican-American War coincided with an event that would be just as impactful for California society: the discovery of gold at Sutter's Mill in January 1848. The discovery put into motion an influx of fortune seekers. Those who arrived first from outside of California came south from the Oregon territory, north from Sonora, east from Hawai'i or north from Peru and Chile along the sea trading routes. Indigenous miners worked the goldfields as well. Some were laborers brought by ranchers to work their claims; Sutter himself brought over one hundred Indigenous laborers from his vast ranch to work in the goldfields for him. Other Indians worked independently "with great energy" to mine for gold, an enterprise that required no capital to begin.[158]

More people arrived the following year, giving the name forty-niners to the immigrant gold seekers. News spread to the Far East; California earned the name Gum San, or Gold Mountain, in Chinese. Miners from Mexico, Peru and Chile brought with them mining experience and methods of separating sand from gold that were quickly adopted by newcomers to the goldfields, and miners informally adopted Mexican mining law that had existed in California prior to the war. Under these laws, the claim to a parcel of land could be "staked" by a prospector, but that claim was valid only as long as it was being actively worked.[159]

An estimated three hundred thousand people came to California during the gold rush, rapidly transforming the demographics of the territory in the north. The port of San Francisco, a small settlement of about two hundred residents in 1846, had grown to a town of about thirty-six thousand by 1852. Men left their homes and employment in droves to pan for gold. In 1848, in a letter to his brother Abraham in Massachusetts, Temple lamented,

> *I am again in the territory of the United States, but it will be a long time if ever, before good order can be enforced in this territory on account of the unequalled quantity of gold that has been found, the enticement is so great that it will be impossible (in my opinion) to enforce laws that may be made, as the regular soldiers will desert.*[160]

One forty-niner described the masts of hundreds of idle ships in the San Francisco harbor that had been abandoned by their crews as "the strangest sight of society I ever saw."[161]

Approximately two-thirds of the forty-niners were white Americans from the eastern United States. They began seeking ways to maximize their advantages at the expense of miners of color.[162] In 1850, the California legislature passed a Foreign Miners' Tax that required miners who were not U.S. citizens to pay twenty dollars a month (later reduced to four dollars a month) for the right to mine in the state. In reality, the tax was collected from only Chinese and Latino miners, while European miners were not forced to pay it.[163] As it turned out, native-born Californios were often assessed the tax as "foreigners" as well. Pérez Rosales, a Chilean forty-niner, recalled that Latinos were lynched, beaten, robbed and burned out in the mining camps.[164] White miners viewed the "foreigners" as taking jobs and places that should more rightly go to Americans. In an environment of increasing xenophobia, Latinos—whether they were native Californios, Sonorans, Peruvians or Chileans—were reduced in the eyes of white miners and settlers to a single group: Mexicans, or, more often in a common pejorative term of the day, "greasers."[165]

As more gold-seekers continued to pour into the creeks and hills along the foothills of the Sierra Nevada mountains, they attacked the Indigenous people, pushing them off their homelands.[166] Numerous massacres are recorded. In 1850, more than sixty Humboldt Indians were killed as they slept in their village because the land they occupied was believed to be rich in gold. Historian Malcolm Rohrbough noted that "the 49ers brought racism and intolerance with them, along with everything else."[167]

The impact of the gold rush was felt differently in the northern and southern parts of the territory. In the north, the white American population rapidly overtook the Californio population, resulting in dispossession of land and a decline in cattle ranching. In the south, the driving of cattle north to feed the miners gave an impetus to the local rancho economy. Cattle whose hides had been selling for two dollars each now commanded thirty to fifty dollars a head when sold for meat. Social relations in the south continued for a period much as they had prior to the war, with Spanish continuing to be the predominant language used at home, in business transactions and in the courts.

U.S. Land Commission and the Struggle to Retain Land Titles

The gold rush got underway when California was a territory of the United States. However, with the rapid influx of American miners and settlers, California was able to move to statehood relatively quickly. In preparation, delegates from ten districts in the territory were elected by popular vote to assemble in Monterey and work on constructing a state government. Of the forty-eight men who assembled in Colton Hall that fall, eight of them were native Californios and six were foreign-born European immigrants; the rest were white Americans. Deliberations and committee work were in English, with translators available for the Spanish-speaking delegates.[168] Several sections in the state constitution showed Mexican influence. For example, all laws were required to be published in both Spanish and English. California also adopted the concept of community property, in which married women had joint ownership of property along with their husbands, as they had under Mexican law.[169]

The delegates grappled with the issue of citizenship. Mexico had granted rights of citizenship to "civilized" Indians and Black people, and the Treaty of Guadalupe Hidalgo ensured that Mexican citizens would have the opportunity to become citizens of the United States. Following American prejudices of the day, however, the delegates advanced language that excluded Indigenous people and African Americans, granting citizenship to "every white, male citizen of Mexico who shall have elected to become a citizen of the United States."[170]

One of the pressing issues facing the new state was the validation of rights to landownership. As described earlier, the Treaty of Guadalupe Hidalgo contained language granting Mexican citizens the "free enjoyment of their liberty and property" but fell short of ensuring that land claims granted under the Mexican government would be recognized. A process was set up with the passing of the California Land Act of 1851 through which landowners could present their claims for validation. In the meantime, the U.S. government declared Indigenous lands public domain, and in 1853 the state government passed legislation enabling squatters to take over Mexican and Spanish land grants and Indigenous lands with "unverified titles"—that is, titles that had not yet been verified as valid.[171] Because of the length of time that the validation process took—on average seventeen years—squatters settled on some rancho lands that ultimately were validated.

During the period from 1852 to 1856, the Land Commission received a total of 813 claims, of which 604 were eventually confirmed for patent. The vague wording or informal establishment of boundaries under Spanish and Mexican rule resulted in denial of claims and loss of property for over 200 of the claimants. Jonathan Temple was required to validate his land claim along with other rancheros. He was required to produce evidence of the validation by the Mexican government of the Nieto family heirs' claim to the Los Cerritos property and of his purchase of the property from each one of the heirs. Temple submitted his grant in 1852, and it was likely approved in the 1850s; however, the final patent for the property was not obtained until after his death, in 1867.[172]

Although the process was onerous and lengthy, Temple's ultimate success was aided by his familiarity with the American legal system and his facility in English as well as his financial standing, which permitted his payment of legal fees over multiple years. Many Californio rancheros, without those advantages, were not as successful. Many were forced to sell their land to pay legal fees, even when they received a positive ownership result. Others found that they could not evict squatters who had taken over their land, even with a land title in hand. María Amparo Ruíz de Burton, in her novel *The Squatter and the Don*, first published in 1885, took up the theme of the injustices suffered by Californios at the hands of squatters, a situation with which she had firsthand experience.

Secularization of the missions during the Mexican era had displaced most of the Indigenous workers and families living at the missions. A few Indigenous families, nonetheless, had managed to maintain control of their property.[173] Under the American land claim process, however, no Indigenous claims were made due to unfamiliarity with the English language and American legal system, and thus no Indian land claims were recognized.

The experience of Rogerio Rocha, who was born at Mission San Fernando in 1801, provides one example of how Indigenous landowners were stripped of their property.[174] After secularization of the missions, Rocha obtained a small plot of land near the mission where he resided for sixty years. The land was part of the holdings of the de Celis family, whose original land grant specified that none of the Indians occupying the land were to be disturbed. When they sold their property to two Americans in 1875, they were assured that this condition of the sale would be respected. However, the new owners later brought suit to evict Rocha and his wife, both of whom were over eighty years old. In the winter of 1886, the couple were placed in a cart and moved two miles to a public road, where they were left along with their possessions. The eviction took place during a four-day rainstorm, and Rocha's wife contracted pneumonia from which she did not recover. Rocha spent his final years on a small patch of land lent to him by a friend.

Tongva elder Craig Torres shared a similar family story regarding his ancestor Prospero, a Gabrielino Indian who had worked as a vaquero at Mission San Gabriel and been given a twenty-three-acre plot of land in recognition of his service.[175] Oft-repeated family stories described how Torres's great-grandmother, Prospero's daughter Candelaria Dominguez, had been swindled out of the property by two Americans who got her drunk and persuaded her to sign away the property with her X on the deed. Torres described how he was able to search through old maps and documents to verify that Prospero had indeed owned a piece of land that is currently part of the Huntington Library estate and that Benjamin Wilson had been the one involved in the takeover of Candelaria's land. "Don Benito" Wilson, as he was known, was a native of Tennessee who became a naturalized citizen of Mexico, married into a prominent Californio family and acquired Rancho Jurupa and numerous other properties in California in addition to the Torres ancestor's plot of land.

Temple's Role in the Growth of the Pueblo

At Rancho Los Cerritos after statehood, cattle ranching continued as it had prior to the war with Mexico and became more lucrative through the sale of cattle to feed miners in the goldfields. John Temple expanded his ranching interests, purchasing Rancho El Tejón with Antonio Del Valle in 1857. This rancho most likely served as a stopping point for herds being driven north. He purchased Rancho El Consuelo in Tulare County as well. He had an interest in sailing ships plying the coast between San Francisco and Acapulco and purchased four hundred miles of coastal property between Acapulco and Mazatlán. During the 1850s, he was considered one of the wealthiest men in Southern California, matched only by his neighbor and compatriot Abel Stearns. Temple's contemporary, Los Angeles merchant Harris Newmark, described him as a "very rich, if miserly, man."[176]

Unlike fellow New Englander Abel Stearns, who was at one point expelled from Alta California when the political faction he backed lost its bid for power and who later represented Los Angeles in the California constitutional convention of 1849, Temple did not demonstrate much involvement in local politics, notwithstanding his participation in vigilantism. He did, however, merge his business interests with community needs to support development in the pueblo of Los Angeles. In 1857, Temple constructed the city's first substantial business building, the two-story brick building known as the Temple Block. This mercantile building housed numerous stores, including Hellman's stationery and bookstore, Rodriguez's grocery store and Lamson's liquor store. The Wells, Fargo & Co. Express offices were also located there.[177] Temple planted pepper trees in front of his store on Main Street and had the idea of using a mixture of tar and sand to cover the bricks in front to form a sidewalk. Unfortunately, the tar would get sticky in the summer heat, proving an impediment to comfortable walking.[178]

In 1859, Temple negotiated with the city government to build the more grandiose Market House, fashioned after Faneuil Hall in Boston, which he rented to the city. The building was occupied by storefronts on the main floor and a meeting hall and theater on the second floor. The city council used the building, topped with its distinctive clock tower, as both the city market and city hall. Newmark provides a less than glorious description of the clock:

> *A striking feature of this market building was the town clock, whose bell was pronounced "fine-toned and sonorous." The clock and bell, however, were*

Market House, built by John Temple in 1859, with its iconic clock tower. *Courtesy of the California History Room, California State Library, Sacramento, California.*

SPRING ST

destined to share the fate of the rest of the structure which, all in all, was not very well constructed. At last, the heavy rains of the early sixties played havoc with the tower, and toward the end of 1861 the clock had set such a pace for itself regardless of the rest of the universe that the newspapers were full of facetious jibes concerning the once serviceable timepiece.[179]

At about this time, Temple joined with other local citizens in the formation of the Library Association, of which he was elected president. A reading room was set up in Stearns's Arcadia Block with books donated from various individual collections, and a monthly fee of one dollar was charged. Unfortunately, the library was not well patronized, and the venture was abandoned.[180]

Temple also was a key player in organizing the first survey of the pueblo in 1849 for the purpose of granting vacant lots for sale from public lands. He was on the committee that hired Edward Ord to complete the survey, and on completion of the map, Temple loaned the city $3,000 to pay for the survey. Apparently, Temple felt the need to supervise the work as well. Ord's assistant, William Hutton, complained,

One day he said to me, pointing to a stone at one corner of a square, "Well, you must come here again; here is only one stone; there must be four." I did not say anything, but pointed to the three others, which were plain enough to be seen, only he was looking the wrong way for them. He did such things several times.[181]

Hutton's impressions of Temple seemed to align with Newmark's description of him as "miserly."

Temple operated as a moneylender in Los Angeles in a period when there were no banks. His neighbor Pedro Domínguez sought a loan to finance an expedition to the goldfields, where he hoped to recoup enough money to pay off his debts. He borrowed $2,000 from Temple, agreeing to an interest rate of 100 percent over a six-month period. In exchange he gave Temple a mortgage against one-half interest in Rancho San Pedro. He took out a second loan, canceling the first, which he was ultimately unable to pay back. As a result, in 1850, Domínguez signed away his portion of Rancho San Pedro, approximately eight thousand acres, using half of the proceeds to pay off his debt to Temple.[182]

In another instance, Temple foreclosed on the mortgage of Juan Bouet, a French merchant who had borrowed money, and seized his two-room adobe house and land. In this instance, however, Temple was connected to Bouet through bonds of compadrazgo, since Temple and his daughter Francisca had served as godparents to Bouet's son. As understood in Spanish, these bonds are between not only godparent and child but also the child's parents and the godparents. They are compadres (literally "co-parents"), and the tie is a significant one. Many of the foreigners who had married into Californio families, such as Pliny Temple and Abel Stearns, served as godparents multiple times, as did their wives. There was an expectation that wealthier families would serve as godparents to their poorer employees or neighbors. Rafaela Temple herself was recorded as godmother to numerous children. In John Temple's case, however, the Bouet family represents the single instance in which he served as godparent, and he did not let that relationship bar him from foreclosing on his compadre and forcing him to declare bankruptcy.

Through his son-in-law Gregorio de Ajuria, Temple expanded his interests in Mexico and, in 1856, was co-partner in the operation of La Casa de Moneda, the national mint, in Mexico City. Ajuria had supported the revolt of Ignacio Comonfort against the Mexican government. With Comonfort's success and his assumption of the presidency, Ajuria was in a position to broker a partnership for his father-in-law in the lease to operate the mint. Although Comonfort's regime was short-lived, and both he and Ajuria and his family fled the country, Temple retained the lease. The mint was operated by Temple's heirs until the Mexican government nationalized the facility in 1893.[183]

Daguerreotype of Francisca Temple de Ajuria with her husband, Gregorio, and their first child, circa 1852. *Rancho Los Cerritos Collection.*

Ajuria took Francisca and their children to France, where their fourth child was born in 1858. With their grandchildren now in France, it is probably no coincidence that this is the year John and Rafaela decided to make their European tour, returning to Los Angeles the following year.

Another facet of Temple's life is revealed in the 1855 diary of one of his contemporaries, William Wallace. Wallace described the spiritualist circle in which he and "Old Mr. Temple" were involved. He described Temple as a healing and magnetizing medium and a man of great wealth, "which he has amassed by industry and economy. His habits have been very pecunious. Since he interested himself in this subject, his friends barely recognize him as the same man. And many of them even say he is crazy." Wallace wrote that Temple would visit persons in the city for the purposes of magnetizing them with violent and rapid manipulations. "Though at first many laughed at the hideous appearance of the old man, yet the results of his efforts were so beneficial that he was looked upon as possessed of wonderful power."[184]

Temple and his circle were part of the Spiritualism movement that achieved prominence in the United States in the latter part of the nineteenth century. By the end of the Civil War, a reported eleven million people subscribed to Spiritualism and thirty-five thousand were practicing mediums. Temple was apparently one of those in the movement known as spiritualist doctors who subscribed to the ideas of Anton Mesmer, believing that the body was governed by a magnetic fluid and when an imbalance occurred, it could cause all manner of ailments.[185] Although nationwide, women were in the forefront of the movement, Temple's circle included men only. There is no record of what Rafaela's thoughts on the matter or on her husband's transformation might have been.

Decline of the Rancho Economy

Although the cattle economy received a boost with the population boom of the gold rush, ranchos were hard-hit in the 1860s by alternating years of flooding and drought. Newmark provides a compelling firsthand account:

> *Following a dry year, and especially a fearful heat wave in October which suddenly ran the mercury up to one hundred and ten degrees, December witnessed heavy rains in the mountains inundating both valleys and towns. On the fourth of December the most disastrous rain known in the history of the Southland set in, precipitating, within a single day and night, twelve inches of water; and causing the rise of the San Gabriel and other rivers to a height never before recorded and such a cataclysm that sand and debris were scattered far and wide. Lean and weakened from the ravaging drought through which they had just passed, the poor cattle, now exposed to the*

> *elements of cold rain and wind, fell in vast numbers in their tracks. The bed of the Los Angeles River was shifted for, perhaps, a quarter of a mile. Many houses in town were cracked and otherwise damaged, and some caved in altogether.*[186]

With the rivers and grasslands drying up due to drought, cattle were not able to survive. Temple decided to sell Rancho Los Cerritos and retire with his wife in San Francisco. He sold the Cerritos rancho to Flint, Bixby & Co., a sheep ranching operation in the Monterey area, for $20,000.

Temple died in 1866 at age seventy, soon after the sale of the rancho and the move to San Francisco. In his will he left all his interests in Mexico, including the operation of the mint, to his daughter and left all his property in the United States to his wife. Rafaela made use of the services of her brother-in-law, Augustus Hinchman, to sell all the property. She traveled to Paris to join her widowed daughter, Francisca, and Francisca's children, residing in Paris until her death in 1887.

The end of the cattle ranching period marked the end of what later writers would refer to as the "halcyon days" of pastoral California. Such descriptions perpetuated a romanticized view of the days of the "Spanish dons," when life was leisurely and gracious but ultimately relegated to the past, incompatible with progress and Americanization.[187] The legacy of the "Spanish fantasy past," during the early years of the twentieth century, inspired California architecture, place-names and pageants as well as serving to denigrate Mexican residents and exclude them from the "Spanish" past. At the Rancho, the mission style of architecture, which is one manifestation of California's romanticized past, would appear as a guiding element in the remodeling of the adobe home in 1930.

CHAPTER 5

SHEEP RANCHING AT RANCHO LOS CERRITOS

In 1866, as we have seen, John Temple sold Rancho Los Cerritos to Flint, Bixby & Co., marking the end of cattle ranching at the Rancho and the beginning of the sheep ranching period. The story of the cousins who formed the company begins, however, well before 1866. Like many others of the period, they were initially lured to California by the discovery of gold and the opportunity of making their fortunes in the goldfields.

"Seeing the Elephant"

In 1849, Benjamin Flint left the small town of New Vineyard, Maine, and joined the migration of Argonauts headed for the goldfields of California. The Argonauts in Greek mythology were those who sailed in search of the Golden Fleece; in the United States, the term became widely used to refer to those who set out in search of gold in California. Most of the Argonauts, although by no means all, were young men.[188] In seeking gold, many were also attracted by the independence and adventure that the journey offered. They set off with hopes of "seeing the elephant," a popular phrase at the time that meant seeing wondrous sights and gaining experience of the world.[189] During the gold rush, it also became associated with disillusionment when the "elephant" was not revealed to be as exciting or profitable as anticipated.

Handbill and newspaper advertisements like this one lured Argonauts to the goldfields. *Public domain.*

Two years later, in July 1851, Benjamin was joined by his younger brother Thomas and his cousins Lewellyn and Amasa Bixby. Their trip to California, made by steamship and then across the Isthmus of Panama and on to San Francisco, lasted fifty-three days. Dr. Thomas Flint wrote in his diary, "We were deck passengers and slept under an awning over the quarter deck in

The mining town of Volcano during the gold rush. *Library of Congress.*

Standee berths, when we could get them, some large stuffed chairs laid down made me a pretty good substitute for pillows."[190] They then traveled inland to join Benjamin in the mining town of Volcano in Amador County.

Today a California Historical Landmark, present-day Volcano is a quiet town of about one hundred residents; in its heyday in the 1850s, it was the site of seventeen hotels, thirty-five saloons, a theater and a courthouse. The town was the site of the first gold discoveries in Amador County and also of the brief Volcano War, in which the local Indians were driven from the area after being falsely accused of theft.[191]

Lewellyn and Thomas worked in the gold fields for only about a week before going to work in a butcher shop in Volcano.[192] Not long afterward, they purchased the shop. Like many others, they found supplying provisions to the miners to be far more lucrative than the backbreaking work of mining itself. As an example of inflated prices in the mining towns, newly arrived forty-niners might be offered fifty dollars for the pair of boots they were wearing, for which they had paid three dollars before setting off for California.[193]

The following year, Jotham and Marcellus Bixby sailed around Cape Horn to join their brothers and cousins in Volcano. Jotham worked in the gold diggings for three years; however, Lewellyn and the Flint brothers made other plans. Flint wrote that they had "agreed to unite our fortunes for the undertaking of bringing to California sheep and cattle, more for the trip than profit."[194] Sewing their fortunes in gold, worth $3,500 each, into specially designed buckskin jackets, the group sailed back to the East Coast to deposit their funds and begin the purchase of sheep.

Sheep Ranching at Rancho San Justo

After visiting with family, later recounting that they talked about California until their "vocal organs could stand the strain no longer," the partners made plans for returning to California with a herd of sheep. In his diary, Thomas recorded the experience of traveling by train from Maine to Indiana and then by horseback across Ohio as they collected and sheared sheep, staying with families along the way. On May 7, he wrote, "Started off for the overland journey with 1,880 sheep, young and old. 11 yoke of oxen, 2 cows, 4 horses, 2 wagons, complete camping outfit, 4 men, 3 dogs and ourselves. Crossed Mississippi River at Keokuk by ferry, $62. Now in Iowa."

Ten months after leaving their homes in Maine, Lewellyn Bixby and the Flints, who had formed Flint, Bixby & Co. for their business venture, arrived in Southern California with about 2,400 sheep. They camped for the winter near the San Gabriel Mission and drove the sheep north the following spring. In 1855, the partners purchased Rancho San Justo near San Juan Bautista in Monterey County jointly with William Hollister, whom they met on the trail coming west. The thirty-four-thousand-acre ranch was originally a Mexican land grant dating from 1839. It was purchased from the second owner, Francisco Pérez Pacheco, for $25,000.[195] The ranch was later partitioned in 1861; Flint Bixby & Co. ended up with the western portion. This rancho served as the headquarters for Flint, Bixby & Co. operations for the next forty years.

In the early 1850s and as a result of the largely male migration to the goldfields, men outnumbered women in California by seven to one.[196] It is not surprising that the Bixby males chose to return to their home state when it came time to consider marriage. In 1859, Lewellyn returned to Maine. His cousin commented in a letter, "If he comes back without [a wife] he will catch many a rub." Lewellyn did marry Sarah Hathaway, whom he met at a party in the home of her father, the Reverend George Whitefield Hathaway. The couple returned to California to live at Rancho San Justo.

Two years later, Jotham Bixby returned to Maine for a visit. While bringing greetings from his sister-in-law, Sarah, in California, Jotham met and courted her sister, Margaret Hathaway. After Jotham's return to California, Margaret traveled with friends across the Isthmus to California, and the couple were married at Rancho San Justo.

The Flint and Bixby partners constructed a large multifamily house on Rancho San Justo where the three Bixby and Flint families lived. Each family had its own bedroom, bath and sitting room, while the parlor, dining room, kitchen and office were communal areas. The women took turns each month taking charge of housekeeping for the whole group of adults, children and guests.

The families resided communally for the next several years, while Flint, Bixby & Co. expanded their sheep ranching operations with the purchase of several ranchos along the California coast: Rancho Huer Huero in San Luis Obispo County, Rancho San Joaquín or Rosa Morada near Hollister and the Rancho Lomas de Santiago and the eastern part of Rancho Santiago de Santa Ana near Newport Beach.[197]

When company expansion continued with the purchase of Rancho Los Cerritos in Southern California in 1866, Jotham was selected to be manager of the twenty-seven-thousand-acre rancho. He took up residence there with Margaret and their two-year-old son, George. Jotham's brother Marcellus and his family also moved to the Cerritos rancho to start a dairying operation about a mile from the Cerritos adobe home.

Jotham was not a partner in Flint, Bixby & Co. himself when he was selected as manager of the Cerritos. During the cattle ranching years, John Temple and his family did not reside year-round at the rancho. Temple employed a mayordomo, or ranch manager, to oversee operations on a daily basis in his absence. When Jotham and his family arrived, they made the rancho their home on a full-time basis, and Jotham himself served as manager. After three years, he was able to buy a half-interest in ownership of the Cerritos; Flint, Bixby & Co. retained the other half. The Rancho was subsequently operated by the partners under the name J. Bixby & Co.

JOTHAM BIXBY

Jotham Bixby by photographer F.G. Schumacher, Los Angeles, circa 1880s. *Rancho Los Cerritos Collection.*

Jotham Bixby (1831–1917) was the seventh child of twelve born to Amasa and Fanny Weston Bixby in Norridgewock, Maine. Jotham's grandfather Solomon served in the Revolutionary War and soon afterward moved his family to settle along the banks of the Kennebec River in Maine, on the edge of the American frontier. In her memoir *Adobe Days*, Jotham's niece Sarah Bixby Smith described the family's life in rural Maine through stories she had heard from her father, Lewellyn:

> *When he was a little boy, there were no matches and no kitchen stoves, so that his mother had to cook before an open fireplace, and the clothes for all the family were made at home. His mother spun wool from their sheep and wove it into cloth and dyed it in the great indigo pot that stood when she was not using it just inside the shed door.*[198]

When he was twenty-one, Jotham decided to join his brothers and cousins in the California goldfields. After working independently in the Volcano diggings and later with them in the sheep business, he met and married Margaret Hathaway. Sarah Bixby Smith recounted that her uncle, when he was eighty, "told me emphatically that his wife not only had been the most beautiful woman in California, but that she still was."[199]

Jotham and Margaret continued to reside at the Rancho until 1881. They eventually had seven children, of whom five survived into adulthood. Their eldest son, George, later assisted Jotham in his business interests and supervised operations at the Rancho after the family moved, first to Los Angeles and then to the fledgling town of Long Beach.

THE HATHAWAY FAMILY

Margaret Hathaway (1843–1927) was the fifth of eight children born to the Reverend George Whitefield Hathaway and his wife, Mary Locke Hathaway. Mary died soon after the birth of her eighth child, also named Mary, and the following year George married her sister Anne. The Hathaway family includes among its ancestors William Bradford, who arrived in America on the *Mayflower* in 1620.

Reverend Hathaway was a Congregational minister and a local leader in the temperance movement and antislavery causes. He served as an army chaplain in the Civil War and was a noted abolitionist who "braved a disapproving crowd by inviting suffragist and abolitionist Lucy Stone to speak to his congregation."[200] The family home in Skowhegan, Maine, was part of the Underground Railroad, a network of secret routes and safe houses operated to assist enslaved people in reaching freedom. Primarily operated by free and enslaved African American abolitionists, the Underground Railroad was supported by white abolitionists as well. The "railroad" was neither underground nor an actual railroad. Rather, it allowed enslaved individuals to disappear from sight as they were conducted from one safe house to the next until they reached a destination in which they could live in freedom. Approximately seventy-five homes and churches in Maine were "depots" on the Railroad, from which "passengers" could escape to Canada.

Reverend Hathaway and his family's abolitionist work in Maine was mirrored by abolitionist activity carried out by free people of color in California. A German visitor wrote that local African Americans "exhibit a great deal of energy and intelligence in saving their brothers" by helping enslaved people to attain freedom in California, which had entered the union as a so-called free state. Mary Ellen Pleasant, a wealthy free woman of color, responded to the passing of California's Fugitive Slave Act by actively seeking out and rescuing enslaved people in rural areas of the state.[201]

Margaret Hathaway Bixby circa 1864. *Courtesy of Long Beach Public Library.*

In addition to its support of abolitionist and temperance causes, Margaret's family was one that valued education and reading. Sarah described her mother, Margaret's sister, as a "high-bred New England lady" and her childhood home as filled with books.[202] They owned classics by Shakespeare, Dickens, Thackeray and Scott and subscribed to the *New York Times* and magazines such as *Harper's*. Sarah said she had the advantage of growing up in a home "where everyone found his chief pleasure and amusement in reading."[203]

At Rancho Los Cerritos, Margaret was responsible for overseeing the running of the household and the education of her young children. She had the help of servants and the support of her sister Susan, who had come to California and traveled south from the San Justo to stay with Margaret and her family.

In 1873, Susan married John Bixby, a younger cousin of Jotham and Lewellyn, who had come from Maine to help supervise the sheep ranching operation on the Cerritos rancho. The couple settled in Wilmington, the nearest town to Rancho Los Cerritos at the time, while John continued to

Opposite: The Hathaway sisters, Mary (*seated*), Susan (*left*), Martha (*center*) and Margaret (*right*), circa 1870. *Rancho Los Cerritos Collection.*

Right: Sarah Bixby as a child. *Rancho Los Cerritos Collection.*

work on the Cerritos. In 1878, John and Susan Bixby leased a portion of nearby Rancho Los Alamitos and moved into the adobe ranch house there.

While Margaret had her sister Susan living close by, first in Wilmington and later at the Alamitos rancho, she was also joined in 1877 by her sister Martha and their father, the Reverend Hathaway. Several months after his second wife died, Reverend Hathaway and Martha decided to leave their home in Skowhegan to join the family at the Cerritos rancho. The following year, Lewellyn and his family moved south from the San Justo to take up residence in the pueblo of Los Angeles. Lewellyn managed the Flint, Bixby & Co. operations, including the Coast Line Stage Company, in Southern California. Thus, all the surviving Hathaway sisters were reunited in Southern California.

Lewellyn's first wife, Sarah, had died after six years of marriage, and Lewellyn had then married Sarah and Margaret's youngest sister, Mary.

Their oldest child was named Sarah, in memory of her mother's sister. Sarah spent summers and holidays during her childhood at Rancho Los Cerritos and in 1925 published a memoir, *Adobe Days*, which included descriptions of a child's view of rancho life.

The Hathaway sisters' families, doubly connected through marriage to Bixby brothers and cousins, were particularly close, and holidays were celebrated together. The families took turns hosting Thanksgiving, Christmas and New Year's Day; however, the Cerritos was the usual site of the Fourth of July celebrations:

> *Cerritos claimed the Fourth of July most often, for its bare courtyard offered a spot free from fire hazard. What a satisfying supply of fireworks our combined resources offered! There were torpedoes, safe for babies, firecrackers of all sizes, double-headed Dutchmen, Chinese bombs—to make the day glorious.*[204]

Sheep Ranching at the Cerritos

During the 1860s, with growing numbers and improved breeds of sheep, California wool production rose from two million to over eleven million pounds per year. The Civil War, which began in 1861, had served as a stimulus to the wool industry in the West because cotton from the South was no longer readily available and the war-torn East was unable to meet the demand for wool. This expanding market had no doubt played a role in Flint, Bixby & Co.'s decisions to expand operations with the purchase of additional ranch lands.

The raising of sheep had begun in California during the Spanish colonial period; however, the mission sheep produced only two to two and a half pounds of wool per shearing. The Bixbys were among later wool growers in the state who imported other breeds of sheep to improve local strains. The Bixbys imported Spanish and French Merino sheep, which had a heavier fleece than the older local breeds. By the end of the decade, a sheep produced an average of six and a half pounds of wool per shearing.[205]

At Rancho Los Cerritos, sheepherders cared for about twenty-five thousand sheep. Many of the sheepherders were Basque immigrants. It is often assumed that Basques were successful sheepherders because they brought experience and skills in the care of sheep from their native region; this may be largely a myth. Basques began arriving in California in numbers, like many other groups, during the gold rush. Mainly young, unmarried males, they sought employment herding sheep in part because it did not require special skills or command of the English language. They did not have experience in open-range sheep herding as practiced in the West. They did bring, however, the experience of a rural upbringing that gave them some skill in caring for livestock, a propensity for hard work and a willingness to undergo extreme hardship in order to advance financially.[206] They often began as wage laborers, saving money to enable them to acquire their own herds. Economic historian Iker Saitua contends that as Basques gained a reputation as "good sheepherders," they also benefited from societal prejudices that favored white immigrant groups over non-white ethnic groups.[207]

The life of the sheepherder involved long periods of isolation. Each herder, assisted by his dogs, took care of about two thousand sheep, herding them from one pasture area to another as they foraged for food. Sheepherders stayed with their herds, camping in wagons or staying in small cabins spread across the range. At the Cerritos, they were brought a basket of food, tobacco and mail each week. One of the Bixby cousins tending sheep at the San Justo tried to discourage his brother from joining them: "If you were to come down here and tend sheep, you could not get but $30 per month, and be obliged to work hard every day, rain or shine, hot or cold, Sundays not excepted."

Twice a year, in the spring and fall, the sheep were brought in from the range to the rancho corrals for shearing. Sheep shearing was one of the better-paying jobs available to ranch workers, but it was seasonal work. Shearers worked in large bands, traveling from one ranch to another. Many of the shearers had previously worked on cattle ranches before these gave way to sheep ranching.

As a young visitor to the Cerritos, Sarah Bixby described the arrival of the sheep shearers:

> *Shearing began on Monday morning, and on Sunday the shearers would come in, a gay band of Mexicans on their prancing horses, decked with wonderful silver-trimmed bridles made of rawhide or braided horsehair, and saddles with high horns, sweeping stirrups, and a wide expanse of beautiful tooled leather.*[208]

The fine detail in Sarah's description permits us to form a mental picture of the arrival of the shearers. However, her use of the term "Mexicans" to describe

Sheep shearers pose for a photograph at the Rancho, 1872. *Rancho Los Cerritos Collection.*

Jotham Bixby supervising the sheep dip after shearing, 1872. *Rancho Los Cerritos Collection.*

the workers, although common in the period, is somewhat misleading. In her study of late-nineteenth-century San Juan Capistrano, historian Lisbeth Hass writes that Anglo-Americans in Southern California tended to understand racial identities based on a polarized notion of white/Mexican.[209] This usage obscures the reality that the "Mexican" group in fact included Californios whose families had resided for several generations in California (including prior to the existence of the country of Mexico) as well as Spanish-speaking Indigenous people and more recent immigrants from Mexico.

The shearers were given space to sleep and store their saddles in the barns during their time at work on the rancho. A shearer clipped the sheep with scissor-like shears, shearing twenty-five to thirty sheep per day. After the sheep were sheared, they were thrown into a long trough filled with a mixture of water, tobacco juice and sulfur and forced to swim to the end while their heads were dunked. The foul mix helped prevent scabies (mites)

Stereograph (stereopticon photograph) by William Godfrey of the Bixby family in the Rancho courtyard, 1872. *Rancho Los Cerritos Collection.*

and skin infections, to which the sheep were particularly susceptible because of small nicks in their skin acquired during shearing.

On the Cerritos rancho, the wage paid to the shearer for each fleece varied with the market value of wool. In good times, Jotham Bixby paid as much as $0.10 to $0.12 per fleece; however, $0.05 to $0.06 per fleece was most common. On occasion, shearers received less. Workers' wages of $0.05 to $0.06 per fleece can be compared with the $1.20 to $2.30 that the Rancho owners received for the sale of each fleece. The sheep business was profitable enough that Flint, Bixby & Co. was able to earn back the $20,000 that was paid for the Cerritos property in just two "clips," or shearing seasons. It would not be for close to one hundred years before agricultural workers, specifically excluded from the federal National Labor Relations Act of 1935, would achieve the right to form unions and strike for better working conditions in California.[210] The sheep industry in the United States to the present day has resisted efforts to improve the demanding and low-paid working conditions of its non-unionized workers.

In 1872, Jotham contracted Los Angeles photographer William Godfrey to visit and photograph the Rancho.[211] Like so many others, Godfrey had come to California from his native state, Michigan, to seek his fortune in the goldfields. Trained as a dentist, he had learned to make daguerreotypes as a side job. In Hangtown, California, he had the opportunity to purchase photographic equipment from a fellow Argonaut. He subsequently worked as a professional photographer, first in San Francisco and later in Los Angeles. In his studio, he produced portraits and cartes de visite (small photographs printed on a card the size of a calling card), but he also produced stereos, double photograph cards intended for use in stereopticons that permit a 3D vision of a scene or locale. Among the many stereos taken by Godfrey are photos of the missions and of early Los Angeles, including the Temple Block. The informal photos taken at Rancho Los Cerritos differ from the more formal studio portraits of the day and provide an invaluable look at rancho work and everyday life.

Juan Cañedo

After the flood and droughts of the early 1860s that decimated the herds, the cattle industry in California did not recover. Many ranchos were sold, and many of the ranch laborers were forced to seek other work. At the Cerritos rancho, a few of the ranch hands who had worked for John Temple were retained at the Bixby sheep ranch. A leader among these was vaquero Juan Cañedo. Former tenants of the rancho later recalled Cañedo, referring to him as the "old Indian."[212]

In *Adobe Days*, Sarah describes Juan Cañedo as a "most perfect" horseman and expert in the use of the reata (rope), "easily superior to those exhibiting in the wild west shows."[213] She claims that Juan said, probably jokingly, that he had been sold with the ranch. When Jotham and Margaret's son George was four years old, Juan taught him to ride a horse on a saddle made especially for the little boy. Juan never used English, although he most likely understood the language, and he served as a teacher of Spanish to the children. Sarah concluded, "George knew and loved Old Juan as long as he lived, provided for his old age, stayed with him when he died, and for many years paid the widow's grocery bill."[214]

Ah Ying and Ah Fan

Like many other ranchers of the period, the Bixbys employed Chinese cooks to prepare meals for the family and the ranch hands, two different meals three times a day. In addition to cooking, they were responsible for doing the laundry for the family and workers. Ah Ying and Ah Fan appear on the 1880 census; however, little is known about their lives prior to coming to work at the Rancho. Although the great majority of Chinese immigrants to California were single men, some had left wives and children in China prior to coming to America.

Chinese immigration to California began—as it had for so many others, including the Bixby family themselves—with the gold rush. In 1852, twenty thousand people made the steamship trip from Hong Kong to San Francisco, a trip that could last from forty-five days to three months.[215] Many borrowed the money for the thirty- to fifty-dollar ticket price from associations

Stereograph of two Rancho workers, most likely Ah Ying and Juan Cañedo, in the courtyard, 1872. *Rancho Los Cerritos Collection.*

representing the Chinese districts from which immigrants hailed. These district associations provided support for new arrivals on their way to the gold fields. The majority of Chinese immigrants considered themselves sojourners, intending to make their fortunes and return home.[216] Many ended up staying much longer than anticipated, sending money to support families in China.

Chinese miners encountered resentment on the part of white miners, particularly as competition for claims grew more intense. Some towns voted to expel the Chinese miners; those who remained were subject to the Foreign Miners' Tax. Those who left the gold fields took work, typically at wages less than those offered to white workers, building bridges and roads. In 1854, the California Supreme Court established that Chinese people had no right to testify against white citizens in court, making them vulnerable to abuse and "ugly anti-Chinese violence."[217]

Later, with labor shortages exacerbated by the Civil War, thousands of Chinese workers were recruited for construction of the Central Pacific Railroad. They were faced with the dangerous and backbreaking work of blasting tunnels and constructing bridges and rail lines through the Rockies. With the completion of the transcontinental railroad in 1869, the former railroad construction workers sought jobs as domestic workers, field hands, factory workers and itinerant peddlers.

Resentment against the Chinese continued, particularly on the part of white workers who viewed their livelihoods as compromised by the Chinese workers' willingness to work for wages that were far less than those paid to white workers while at the same time refusing to consume American products.[218] Anti-Chinese riots broke out in California; the deadliest occurred in Los Angeles in 1871. There, a mob of five hundred white and Latino men attacked, robbed and murdered residents of Chinatown after the shooting of a white male by a Chinese man, lynching nineteen immigrant males and shooting several others. The attacks occurred a few blocks from the Market House that had been built and owned by John Temple the decade before.

Subsequent riots occurred in San Francisco and other towns throughout the state. The Workingmen's Party of California, with Dennis Kearney as its president, was one of the most visible anti-Chinese groups to emerge in California. Kearney led an anti-Chinese parade of over ten thousand men through the streets of San Francisco, later carrying his message across the country and making famous the rallying cry, "The Chinese must go!"[219]

The Workingmen's Party acquired political clout, sending a significant number of representatives to the constitutional convention of 1878. Article

XII of the new constitution sought to eliminate the hiring of Chinese workers and to discourage Chinese immigration, with the implicit intent of affecting U.S. immigration legislation. Several of the sections were later not upheld in court; however, federal legislation passed in 1882, the Chinese Exclusion Act, did prohibit all immigration of Chinese laborers for ten years. This act was the first major U.S. law ever implemented to prevent all members of a specific national group from immigrating to the United States.

Ah Ying and Ah Fan had immigrated prior to the Chinese Exclusion Act. The 1880 census lists Ah Ying, single, age thirty-eight, as cook and Ah Fan, single, age twenty-one, as cook/servant. They received room and board as part of their payment; an alcove between the dining room and kitchen served as their sleeping area. No account books from Rancho Los Cerritos have survived; however, ledgers and journals kept by John Bixby at the Alamitos rancho document the Chinese workers and their pay on his ranch during the 1880s. It is likely that wages and conditions at the Cerritos rancho were comparable.

Ah Fan had worked as an apprentice under Ah Ying at the Cerritos rancho, coming to work as head cook at the Alamitos rancho in 1874. Initially he earned thirty-five dollars a month, a wage that had gone up to forty-five dollars a month by 1893. Other Chinese workers at the Alamitos rancho included the assistant cook, Ah Keen, whose pay started at twenty-five dollars a month, and Wo Chung Hong, listed as a laborer/herder, whose pay was thirty-five dollars a month. Since the cooks and herders worked seven days a week, thirty-five dollars a month a would be the equivalent of thirty-six dollars a day in today's dollars. John Bixby also employed workers he listed as "Ditch Chinamen" to excavate a ditch from the San Gabriel River to ensure a steady water supply for the sheep.

Ah Fan was listed as Fan Fong in later census and real estate records. After John Bixby's death in 1881, Fan Fong was one of several ranch workers who invested in lots in the Alamitos Beach development that John had started on the southern portion of Rancho Los Alamitos land. The 1880s saw a land boom in Southern California, prompted by the arrival of the Santa Fe Railroad to Southern California and the resulting price war between the Santa Fe and the Southern Pacific Railroads. As the population grew, the price of property went up as well. Although Fan paid $817 for two lots in the development in 1888, the price had dropped to ten dollars per lot by the time he sold the lots in 1908.[220]

No photographs are available of Ah Ying or Ah Fan, but the archives at Rancho Los Cerritos include the carte de visite photo taken in 1875 of

Carte de visite photograph of Kao Lang, 1875. *Rancho Los Cerritos Collection.*

Kao Lang, the cook who worked for John's oldest brother, Augustus. Carte de visite photographs were often taken to send to relatives in China or in anticipation of a trip. The rancho cooks worked seven days a week with no days off, but some returned to China after several years to visit family. Ah Fan may have been one of these men, since he was listed on the 1900 census as married.

An End to Sheep Ranching at the Cerritos Rancho

The period of sheep ranching at the Cerritos rancho corresponds to the period roughly from 1870 to 1900 that historians have called the Gilded Age. The Gilded Age was one of large-scale industrialization and immigration and rapid economic development in the West. It was an age characterized by the disparity between great fortunes and urban poverty.[221] The term *robber barons* was used to describe wealthy industrialists whose success was attained through unscrupulous and monopolistic business practices. In California by the mid-1870s, the Southern Pacific Railroad's owners, or the "Big Four"—Leland Stanford, Collis Huntington, Mark Hopkins and Charles Crocker—owned 85 percent of all railroad mileage in California. With close to a monopoly on rail travel, the Southern Pacific acquired a reputation for charging "all the traffic will bear"—that is, charging for freight and passengers at the very highest rate possible, thus the term *robber barons*.[222]

The 1870s were a period that saw increasing public concern over land monopolies as well. Large tracts of land under single ownership, many of which had been purchased as former Mexican land grants, were coming under criticism, with calls for limits on the number of acres owned or for higher taxation on the land.[223] In his book documenting the Bixby family and its numerous business interests, Bixby family heir Stephen Dudley states that "Flint, Bixby & Co. had the dubious honor of being included on a list of '22 land grabbers.'"[224] As owners of 334,000 acres among the various ranchos that it had acquired, Flint, Bixby & Co. was one of the largest landowners in the state at this time. While it is the case that the Flints and the Bixbys worked hard and were astute in their investments, they had also benefited from a labor environment in which they could employ non-union workers, many of them persons of color, working long hours under difficult conditions and receiving low wages.

The decade of the 1870s had seen periodic droughts and periods of fluctuation in the price of sheep. As a result, pastureland was diverted for other uses, such as farming and dairying. The Bixby family moved to Los Angeles in 1881 but for several years made two trips to the Rancho each year to oversee the sheep shearing operations. The last big shearing at the Rancho took place around 1886. With the Bixby family no longer in residence and sheep ranching no longer prominent, tenant farmers worked the RLC lands, and tenants rented rooms in the adobe home.

CHAPTER 6

THE TENANT ERA AT THE RANCHO

During the "Tenant Era" of RLC history, parcels of land were leased for farming and dairy operations, and rooms in the adobe house were rented to tenants. This era covers the period between occupation of the adobe by the Jotham Bixby family (ending in 1881) and the remodeling of the house as a single-family residence by Llewellyn Sr. and Avis Bixby (beginning in 1930). The Rancho's tenant era corresponds roughly to the Progressive Era in U.S. history (1890–1920s), a period characterized by a rise in trade union activity to secure better working conditions for laborers and by increasing visibility of the women's suffrage movement, which sought women's right to vote. It was a period of growth in urbanization and of the "first great wave of immigration," in which twenty million immigrants arrived in the United States between 1880 and 1920. Close to one million of these immigrants came north from Mexico during the decade of the Mexican Revolution (1910–1920). The Progressive Era saw advancements in transportation, including automobile and air travel. These national trends are reflected in Rancho history and in the stories of Rancho residents. They include the growth of urbanization on Rancho property with the founding of the city of Long Beach, the subdivision of RLC property for smaller farms and dairies and the renting out of the rancho adobe to tenants, many of whom were Mexican workers and their families.

During the late 1870s, Flint, Bixby & Co. experienced financial difficulties associated with declines not only in the viability of sheep ranching but also in several of its investment ventures. Jotham Bixby and his family moved to

Los Angeles in 1881. Although some sheep ranching operations continued for a few more years, the decision was made to begin selling or leasing parcels of the RLC property.[225] The decade of the 1880s thus saw Rancho Los Cerritos enter a period of transition from large-scale sheep ranching to subdivision for smaller-scale agriculture and dairy operations as well as the sale of land for urban development. The city of Long Beach was founded on Rancho land, followed by Bellflower, Paramount (formerly Clearwater), Signal Hill and Lakewood.

Birth of the City of Long Beach

In 1881, the same year that the Bixby family moved to Los Angeles, Jotham leased four thousand acres in the southwestern corner of Rancho property to English investor William Willmore, giving him the option to buy the parcel after three years. Willmore envisioned the establishment of Willmore City and what he called the American Colony on the outskirts of the city, where plots of land of five to forty acres were to be sold for farms and dairies. Promotion of the proposed city and farming community was done through the California Immigrant Union, an organization established to encourage families from the Eastern United States, Europe and Canada to settle in California. Jotham Bixby himself was a supporter of the Immigrant Union. Willmore City was laid out to include twelve blocks between Magnolia and California Streets and ten blocks from the ocean north. A shady promenade was planned along the bluff overlooking the ocean. Willmore failed to attract a sufficient number of buyers, however, and was unable to pay off the final $100,000 debt to Mr. Bixby.

Willmore's contract was picked up in 1884 by the real estate firm of Pomeroy and Mills, who formed the Long Beach Land & Water Company and spent over $250,000 in improvements to the water system and streets of the planned town. The Long Beach Hotel, which included a public bathhouse, was built along the bluff. The success of the fledgling city, which was renamed Long Beach and incorporated in 1888, was spurred by the real estate "Boom of the Eighties."[226] The arrival in Los Angeles of the Santa Fe Railroad in 1885 to compete with the Southern Pacific Railroad resulted in price wars that brought railroad ticket prices down and stimulated the arrival of new residents to Southern California, mainly from the East and Midwest. Spurred by this population growth and Midwesterners fleeing the Dust Bowl, Long Beach would earn the nickname Iowa by the Sea in later decades.

With increasing popularity as a seaside resort, Long Beach grew from a population of about two thousand in 1900 to fifty-five thousand—a thirty-fold increase—by 1920. The Pike amusement zone was established at the seaside in 1902 and included a grand public bathhouse (the Plunge), the municipal pier and a connecting wooden boardwalk, or pike. Rancho tenant Clarinda Bustamante Carter described how local families enjoyed the beach in the early years:

> *Mother rented a little wagon, and the whole family got inside. In those days they had about fifteen or twenty wagons there. You could rent them for ten cents apiece for two hours. You ran them out in the water. They had a kind of a cover on the wheels. You had your bathhouse right there and nobody would see you, because in those days women never showed their bare legs.*

The city was surrounded by farms and ranches. Portions of nearby Rancho Palos Verdes totaling seventeen thousand acres had been purchased by J. Bixby & Co. in 1882 and operated as a cattle ranch until 1913, when

The shorefront and Pike in Long Beach circa 1900–1920. *Courtesy of Long Beach Public Library.*

the land was sold to real estate developers.[227] The pastoral roots of the city of Long Beach were in evidence in Arthur Davies's recollections of growing up in Long Beach in 1904:

> *They used to run sheep down Anaheim Street from the Fred Bixby Ranch and run 'em over on Palos Verdes hills. We found out later there would be as high as five thousand sheep go down Anaheim Street and they would put up an awful cloud of dust. If kids were on the school grounds, you couldn't hold them. We all went up and watched the sheep go by.*

Jotham Bixby's grandson Richard Bixby, circa 1916. *Rancho Los Cerritos Collection.*

Jotham Bixby's grandson Richard Bixby told a similar anecdote from his adolescence. Richard was the son of George H. Bixby and had grown up in the family home near the Rancho adobe in what is now the Cerritos neighborhood. Richard and his friends used the opportunity of the annual cattle drives from the Palos Verdes Hills to the Los Altos lowlands to dress as cowboys and have some fun. "We'd separate out a pretty good-sized strong calf that still had plenty of pep and run him down Pine Avenue clear to the ocean, scattering people right and left and whooping and hollering, pretending to rope him."

A HISTORY OF FLOODING

A recurring theme in Richard Bixby's memories was the way that water shaped the landscape of early Long Beach. The Mitchell Ranch, slightly north of Cherry Avenue and San Antonio Drive, yielded one of the biggest artesian wells in the area. Artesian wells were numerous, and in the early twentieth century, such wells remained uncapped and flowed along man-made ditches into the river.

The Los Angeles River would periodically flood after winter rains, threatening lives and property. Richard remembered the river spreading out four or five miles wide between the Cerritos mesa and the Dominguez mesa.

An artesian well on RLC property circa 1918. *Rancho Los Cerritos Collection.*

> *People living out in that area had to use rowboats almost every winter to get to higher spots to get out. The same thing held good in that area north of the Virginia Country Club. I remember one experience of riding in one of the Long Beach lifeboats, which we had borrowed to get the people out of trouble. I rode from the foot of the hill at Virginia Country Club entrance as far north as where the flood control bridge is now. We rode right down the middle of the highway. You couldn't see the fence posts—they were underwater—but telephone posts were perhaps sticking up eight or ten feet above the water.*

Richard also recalled several instances from around 1910 of "farmers plowing up their lands and running into skeletons of people who were no doubt drowned during some of those floods that nobody ever knew anything about."

Catastrophic floods, such as the one described by Richard Bixby, were common in times of heavy winter rains throughout the nineteenth and early twentieth centuries. The Los Angeles River emptied its waters not directly into the ocean but rather into vast marshy areas. A saltwater marsh once stretched from the Palos Verdes hills to Long Beach. The river's waters helped make Los Angeles one of the richest agricultural areas in the nation but also caused considerable damage and loss of life as the region became more populated.

Flooding in the winter of 1861–62 may have been the most devastating in California history and signaled the demise of the cattle industry. Flooding occurred yearly during the boom decade of the 1880s, in one instance causing Los Angeles to be isolated for seven days. The great flood of 1914 destroyed houses, roads and bridges and inundated close to twelve thousand acres in Los Angeles County. Some of the channels in the Los Angeles and Long Beach Harbors were rendered unnavigable due to silt deposits.[228]

The 1914 flood spurred action on the part of the City of Los Angeles to address the need to control flood risks. Numerous proposals were put forth in subsequent years, including rechanneling the riverbed, diverting the river from the harbor, building a protective dike and constructing a San Gabriel Canyon dam. However, disagreements over actions to be taken and lack of consistent public support for the bond measures stalled progress on flood control efforts. Following another devastating flood in 1934, the City of Los Angeles requested funding from the Works Progress Administration to address the issue. Work was carried out by laborers on WPA relief rolls under the supervision of the U.S. Army Corps of Engineers, and the reinforced concrete channels that characterize the river today were begun. By 1960, the Los Angeles River, the river that had formed the original boundary of Rancho Los Cerritos, had been refashioned as a "51-mile storm drain."[229]

The Bixby Family and Long Beach

The Jotham Bixby family moved from Los Angeles back to Long Beach in 1886 and in later years occupied a large home on the bluff overlooking the ocean. Jotham remained active in the extensive business interests of the family companies.[230]

The Alamitos Land Co. was formed in 1888 after John Bixby's death by the owners of Rancho Los Alamitos (John Bixby's heirs, in addition to owners William Hellman and J. Bixby & Co. partners Jotham Bixby, Thomas Flint and Lewellyn Bixby). The company subdivided and sold most of the land in Long Beach east of Alamitos Avenue, retaining sections on Signal Hill. An oil well, the Alamitos No. 1, on company land leased to the Shell Oil Company, was the site of the discovery of oil in June 1921. The discovery initiated an oil boom that transformed the character of Signal Hill and doubled the population of Long Beach. By 1930, the population of Long Beach had grown to 142,000—from 55,000 the decade before. Numerous other Bixby companies and real estate ventures included the Loma Vista Ranch Company, the Anaheim Co-operative Sugar Company, the Bixby Land Company, the Jotham Bixby Company and the Palos Verdes Company. Participation of extended family members in a complex web of interconnected business activities and ventures characterized the family enterprises.

Jotham and Margaret were active in the development of Long Beach in its early years. Margaret was a founding member of the First Congregational Church of Long Beach, which was established in 1888 and met in Cerritos Hall, built by the Bixbys on the corner of Third Street and Locust Avenue. At the time, Cerritos Hall was the only public building in Long Beach and was in demand for temperance rallies and religious meetings. The Bixbys gifted the hall and adjoining land to the church. Later, in 1913, Margaret and Jotham donated $25,000 (one-quarter of the projected cost of construction) for the building of a new and larger church on the same site. A church centennial history stated that during inauguration ceremonies, "Mr. Jotham Bixby, called the 'Father of Long Beach,' was honored and presented with

Above: Jotham Bixby family home at 2100 East Ocean Boulevard circa 1915. *Rancho Los Cerritos Collection.*

Right: Lewellyn Bixby in front of Alamitos Land Company headquarters office in Los Angeles in December 1896, two days before he died. *Rancho Los Cerritos Collection.*

an ebony-handled silver trowel." He laid the cornerstone of the building on his eighty-third birthday in 1914.[231] The historic First Congregational Church, with its magnificent rose window dedicated to Jotham and Margaret, continues to serve the community in downtown Long Beach.

Jotham also donated land for several parks in the city. Mark Houghton, who joined the city's engineering department in 1921 and served for thirty-six years, described several of the Bixbys' land donations:

> *The Bixbys had previously dedicated a series of strips along the south side of Ocean Boulevard as a public park. Sometime later, when the Pacific Electric laid a streetcar line out Ocean Boulevard, the Bixbys gave them an encasement to locate the tracks on this portion of the bluff. And still later, when the Pacific Electric moved their tracks, the Alamitos Land Company, the owner of this property, deeded those strips to the City of Long Beach for park purposes, and we now know the area as Bluff Park.*

Today, Bluff Park, overlooking the ocean, is home to the *Lone Sailor* statue that honors all the men and women who have served in the U.S. Navy.

In 1903, the Alamitos Land Company gifted the city with the land for a park known initially as Alamitos Park. After annexation to Long Beach, the park was renamed Jotham Bixby Park in 1907. Located between the present-day Cherry and Junipero Avenues, the park was on the outskirts of the city at the time it was donated. Houghton recounted that "Jotham planted many of the trees in that park and then he tried to persuade the City of Long Beach to lay water lines out there to take care of the cultivation and irrigation of the park." In a letter to the local newspaper, Jotham's sister-in-law Martha Hathaway pointed out that the whole family had contributed to the park and that John Bixby's family "used to come down on Sunday bringing trees on a big, old hayrack wagon and replant them down in the park area."

In 1923, the City of Long Beach purchased 257 acres of land from the Alamitos Land Company for $900,000 for the establishment of Recreation Park. In a later interview, Llewellyn Bixby Jr. described how the deal took place. The city manager and Fred Bixby agreed "with a handshake, nothing written, that they'd sell it to the city for X dollars if the citizens wanted it." Llewellyn's opinion was that "it was a hell of a bargain. Fred made a bad deal for the company and a good deal for the city."

With the sale of park land to the city, the Virginia Country Club, which had been leasing the land for its golf course since its establishment in 1909, was forced to seek a new location. Llewellyn Bixby Sr., an avid golfer, was a charter club member and served as its secretary and treasurer. He was instrumental in helping secure the 133 acres that the country club purchased near the RLC adobe from the Jotham Bixby Company for its new location. The golf course opened for play on September 1, 1921. It may be that the proximity of the country club to his family's historic home prompted Llewellyn Bixby Sr.'s later decision to purchase the deteriorating adobe house and remodel it as his family residence.

FARMS, RANCHES AND DAIRIES

While the city of Long Beach was in the process of development on one area of Rancho property, Jotham Bixby was leasing other parcels to tenant farmers for the cultivation of beans, beets, barley and other crops. The Mitchell Ranch, the Andrews Ranch, the Wardlow Ranch and the Bean Ranch (later to become the Bixby Knolls neighborhood) were among the ranches located on RLC land. Artesian wells, such as the gusher on the Mitchell Ranch described earlier, provided water for the ranches as well as for the city of Long Beach.

Until his death in 1917, Jotham Bixby continued to take an active interest in the various farm enterprises on RLC property. Loretta Berner grew up on the Bean Ranch, where her mother was a cook. Loretta went on to become an amateur historian of Long Beach and an active participant in interviews and presentations at Rancho Los Cerritos. She recalled a story related to Jotham Bixby's overseeing of the ranch work on his property:

> *When Mr. Jotham Bixby got older, I don't know whether he got cranky or what, or whether he just thought the men were wasting his money if they weren't working every time he looked at them. Because if he would find them waiting between loads of hay or something, he would tell Colby Clark, the boss, to lay them off or Mr. Andrews to lay them off—they weren't worth their salt and to get rid of them. So whenever Chet Andrews saw Bixby drive in the road from San Antonio Drive in his horse and buggy and start down the road toward the field, he could see the old man coming. He was called Old Man Jotham, by the way, on the ranches. Anytime they saw the old man coming, Chet Andrews would tell the guys to run and hide until he was gone.*

Jotham Bixby visiting a tenant farm in his horse-drawn buggy circa 1907. *Rancho Los Cerritos Collection.*

Jotham Bixby's habit of being on the job all the time recurred in his grandson Richard's memories as well:

> *I remember when they got his first automobile. He got so that he couldn't drive* [a wagon]. *He always had a high-stepping team, and when his eyesight began to get a little bad, why, he had two or three runaways and they decided to get him an automobile. Well, of course he had a driver, and the very first day out with it, going out to the ranch around Cerritos, he simply pointed to the driver and said, "Go over there where they're plowing. I want to talk with them." The boy said, "Well, I can't drive across that plowed field." "Well," he says, "I don't want this thing then; get me my team of horses!"*

Many of the tenant farms on Rancho property were beet farms. Beet farming required seasonal hand labor during the harvesting process for pulling and topping. In California, this physically demanding and low-paid work was typically done by Chinese workers and later by Japanese and Mexican work gangs.[232] Nellie King Menke, daughter of the manager of King Ranch, recalled how her father would contract workers as needed:

The one who was the foreman of the Mexicans was Juan Lopez. They did beet topping for the ranch, sugar beets. When dad would need them for maybe some extra work, he'd tell Juan to get me some of them to come down and help out with this or that.

Living conditions for the seasonal workers were precarious. Aurelio Arias, whose family had arrived from Mexico in 1903 in search of work, described the housing provided for the workers on one farm: "There were about six families living in one barn. It was converted into a shelter for all of us. We lived the winter in the crowded barn. In the spring and summer, we lived in a tent on the Davis farm."

The beet farmers would transport their sugar beets by field wagons to the railroad cars. Aurelio remembered Alameda Road as being "packed hard by the traffic of five-ton beet wagons and of six-horse teams that traveled back and forth on its dirt surface."

Working and living together, and looking out for one another, was common among farm families. Katherine Bushong, daughter of one of the original surveyors of Willmore City, described visiting back and forth among ranch families in the early years. "I'd look out and look up the road and I'd say, 'Oh, I think the Lewises are coming.' Mama would say, 'I believe it is,' and she'd call Papa and she'd say, 'Go out and kill a couple of chickens.'"

Discussing relations among neighbors, Katherine described their collaborative spirit: "We took care of people. There was no charitable institution in Long Beach, so we just took care of people." She described an incident in which a widow living with her children on a farm north of Willow Street was stranded during a bad flood and ran low on food for her family and her animals. Katherine went to Mrs. Jotham Bixby, at their home on Ocean Avenue, to ask for help.

So she said, "Well, all right then, George will attend to that." And I said, "Well, you will have George right away—see him just as quick as he can because those children out there, they're hungry." And she said, "Well, I'll send him out." And so George H. sent them a cow out and then the horses were underfed by that time and they couldn't get out, so he sent some extra help out and got a load of wood out for her and did all sorts of things.

Multiple dairies operated on Rancho land over the years as well. Charles Mitchell, who was a Bixby relative (the brother of Thomas Flint's wife, Elizabeth Hewitt Flint) and his family lived on Rancho property from 1881

Farm families on the side porch of the Mitchell/Andrews ranch house on RLC land circa 1908. *Rancho Los Cerritos Collection.*

to 1886 and operated a dairy with two hundred cows. He established a cheese factory on a site that later became the township of Clearwater (today the city of Paramount).

Signal Hill was home to fruit, flower and vegetable farms beginning in the early 1900s and was the site of settlement by Japanese farmers beginning in about 1905. Many of the Japanese immigrants had arrived after first working in the sugar plantations of Hawaii, attracted by wages that were significantly higher in California. Land was leased by Japanese "truck farmers" who grew produce and flowers to sell commercially at the old farmer's market in Long Beach. Some of the fields were devoted to flowers such as zinnias, chrysanthemums and gladiolas. In others, strawberries and cucumbers were cultivated, protected by muslin cloth covers that permitted out-of-season harvesting and sale.[233]

As with the Chinese immigrants, who had earlier experienced discrimination and opposition culminating in the Chinese Exclusion Act, the success of Japanese farmers and fishermen led to resentment and retaliation from white citizens. In November 1920, California voters passed the Alien Land Law, which excluded native-born Japanese, the issei generation, from owning land. Although the Alien Land Law did not specify Japanese immigrants, it barred "aliens ineligible for citizenship" from owning land or leasing it for more than three years. Due to previous immigration laws, "aliens ineligible for citizenship" meant Asian immigrants.[234]

Many Japanese farmers were forced out of their Signal Hill farms in the aftermath of the legislation; others left after the discovery of oil on Signal Hill in 1921. Kimi Sugiyama described the effects on local farms of the gushers of oil that fell on the soil and on the white canvas covers for the cucumber beds and the farmers' inability to get compensation from oil companies for their losses. A few of the farms were able to continue until the 1940s, when the internment of the Japanese population during World War II ended the truck farming era.

AIR TRAVEL IN LONG BEACH

Rancho Los Cerritos property was also the site of the first airfield in Long Beach. The first transcontinental flight landed right on the beach in Long Beach in 1911, and the beach continued to be used as a runway until an airport was built. Alfred Valenzuela recounted how his father was approached by local stunt pilot Earl Daugherty about establishing an airfield on the property that Paul Valenzuela leased from Mr. Bixby:

> *There my dad had the ground leased, and he used to run cattle on Willow and Long Beach Boulevard. So Daugherty says, "I'll give you so much for the lease, Paul." And then he says, "Well, I'll sell it to you," and he gave him so much. He says, "Now I want you to clear the land for me so I can put my airport in here. You can clean it out with horses, you know."*

Another tenant farmer, Alfred Encinas, described the excitement of the early air shows:

> *At that time, they were starting to fly a lot of airplanes off of there. We would go up on Sunday to the end of where the barricade was and watch them start out and fly. Sometimes they would come near our head—not too far from us. And sometimes they would land out in the fields. One time there were some beet croppers working out in the field and the plane was coming down to land and they couldn't get there too well, so they started*

Pioneer aviator Earl Daugherty circa 1919. *Courtesy of Long Beach Public Library.*

> *like a bunch of chickens ahead of it—running away from it—the same direction the plane was going. And the plane still landed probably a mile beyond them after it stopped.*

Daugherty Field opened in 1919 at the northeast corner of Bixby Road and Long Beach Boulevard. It was used for air shows, stunt flying and passenger rides, and later became the site of a flight school. In 1923, Daugherty Field became the site of the first municipal airport of Long Beach.

Tenants at the Adobe

Jotham and Margaret Bixby moved to Los Angeles in 1881 with their youngest daughter, Fanny, who was born in 1878. The family moved back to Long Beach in 1885 but chose to make their home in downtown Long Beach rather than residing at the Rancho.

After returning from college in the mid-1880s, George H. Bixby, the oldest son of Jotham and Margaret, moved into the old adobe and assumed management of his father's remaining sheep ranching operations. In 1890,

George H. built a large new home and several farm buildings on La Linda Drive, about a mile south of the adobe. Thereafter, the old house was rented out for various functions. Many of the people who resided there over the next three decades were former employees of the family or of the farms and dairies on RLC property.

Ah Ying, a Chinese cook for the Jotham Bixby family, was one of the workers who continued to live at the Rancho until 1887. Another early resident was William Boyle, who leased part of the house and used it as the headquarters for his dairying operations from about 1894 to 1906. He then moved his operation to newer facilities near today's Forty-Fifth Street and Elm Street.

Boyle employed five or six milkers, each of whom was able to manage about fifty cows. Boyle's story illustrates how Rancho families were interconnected in interesting ways. One of the milkers, who worked for Boyle from 1893 to 1896, was Bert Carter. Carter courted Clarinda Bustamante, who lived in a house nearby, which she described as "by the river, about three blocks. It had pepper trees around it." Clarinda's brother was the chief vaquero for Fred Bixby at Rancho Los Alamitos.

Between 1906 and 1919, families rented out individual rooms in the adobe house. Although many of the renters are unknown, some individual names and stories have been documented and provide glimpses into the lives of residents of the adobe. The Thomas Ricketts family moved into the upstairs bedroom on the south end of the main house in 1906. Thomas worked on various ranches, mostly at the Howard King Ranch in what is now North Long Beach. One of their daughters was born in the upstairs bedroom at the Rancho. The older Ricketts children attended Cerritos School, located on Willow Street. Thomas later worked for Susanna Bixby Bryant at the Bryant Ranch, raising cattle, horses and alfalfa.

A few years later, Ramona López García operated a boardinghouse in the adobe. Family recollections describe her as wearing a gun strapped to her leg and often carrying a shotgun. One of her tenants was Pedro Cortez Rosales, whose parents had immigrated from Zacatecas, Mexico, at the turn of the century. Pedro Rosales had a contract with George H. Bixby to raise sugar beets. Pedro moved into the adobe with his wife, Louisa Garcia Felix, and their children. Their daughter Jenny was born at the Rancho. Jenny later said that she was so small when she was born that her mother put her in a shoebox in the windowsill to get sunlight.

During the same period, Bill and Mary Lerg lived in the large upstairs bedroom in the south end of the main house (where the Ricketts family had

Above: The Ricketts family were tenants living at Rancho Los Cerritos circa 1907. *Courtesy of Long Beach Public Library.*

Left: Boardinghouse manager Ramona López García circa 1917. Ramona is on the horse wearing a pistol and bandolier in this posed studio portrait. *Rancho Los Cerritos Collection.*

lived). Bill Lerg raised and butchered cows and hogs on the ranch for sale in his butcher shop in Long Beach. Bill's nephew Alphonso De Cigaran stayed with the Berg family and slept on a mat in one corner of the bedroom. Alphonso later married and stayed with his wife, Nina, in what he referred to as the "little girls' bedroom." Alphonso remembered that the blacksmith shop in the south wing was used as a hog and chicken pen. His half-brother, Sam Meyer, lived at the Rancho as well and drove a milk truck into Los Angeles from the King Ranch.

Miguel Murillo

The resident who lived for the longest time at the Rancho was Miguel Murillo (sometimes spelled Morillo). Later referred to as the Old Indian, Murillo was of Cahuilla and Californio descent. He was known to have been a very skilled vaquero and teller of tall tales. Miguel's death certificate lists him as born in 1830 at San Juan Capistrano to Brigido Morillo and his wife, Antonia, both of whom were from San Juan Capistrano. In her memoir *Adobe Days*, Sarah Bixby described him as a Temple retainer who was "spending his last days as a tenant of the old house."[235] Miguel passed away in 1931 at age 101.

Miguel was a vaquero who learned to break horses at the Rancho when he was fourteen. Concepción Coronado Liera recalled what he told the Coronado children about his work as a vaquero:

> *He used to sit under the porch and tell us stories of how he used to work with George Bixby and bring cattle from Arizona. Take 'em to the harbor, around Wilmington at the time. Well, he used to run up the cattle from the ranch out here and herd them down to the waterfront to load them up there. I often wondered in my mind what kind of docks or piers they had there. And he said that they had started out with handmade posts in the ground, the water not deep enough so they could float, like a barge or raft, to get those cattle onto the boats. It was too close, too shallow, see, so where this was shallow, they would drive these posts, and that must have been quite a chore to do that.*

Miguel married Antonia Silvas, an Indigenous woman of the Soboba Band of Luiseño Indians, and she worked for the Bixby family as well. Their

Rancho vaquero Miguel Murillo, also known as Uncle Mike, photographed in 1929. *Courtesy of Historical Collections Security Pacific National Bank.*

daughter, Clara Murillo Cline, was born at the Rancho in 1893. Clara remembered there being chickens, cows and horses at the Rancho when she was growing up.

"Uncle Mike," as he was known to the Coronado children who lived at the Rancho in the 1920s, emerges as a larger-than-life personage in the recollections of Rancho tenants. He was a gifted storyteller. Virginia Coronado Babcock described a common scene from her childhood:

> *I can still see—we used to sit back here—there used to be a big rose bush back here—we'd sit out here with him, and he'd tell us all these crazy stories about the ghosts. Then we'd go out front and he'd roll his own cigarettes, you know. He'd roll his own cigarettes and he'd smoke a whole little sack of tobacco telling us all these crazy ghost stories.*

Virginia went on to relate one of the ghost stories that had delighted the children:

> *Uncle Mike used to tell us not to go beyond where the riverbed used to be. There used to be a big bridge over the riverbed. Well, he told us never to go by that bridge, or go over the bridge at five o'clock, because a herd of horses would come through and he says, "You can't see 'em, but you can hear 'em. But you'll never be able to get out of their way."* [Laughter] *So we would never go over the bridge at a certain time.*

According to Uncle Mike, ghosts inhabited the adobe as well:

And the next room had a stairway going down into the—we used to call it the dungeon. There were chains on the wall—with the cuffs, and then they had, I remember, shackles like leg shackles. We were down there just once, because my uncle said that if we ever went in there, we wouldn't be able to get out, 'cause the ghosts would close that door, and there we would be stuck in there, you know.

In Dario Oreña's memoir of his family's ranching experiences in early California, he describes one of the vaqueros, Jesus Arrellanes, who was known for his storytelling skill. Oreña described Arrellanes as "a man with a lively imagination, and the ability to tell at any time a tale, and to make a good story a better one. The men would gather in delight when he was in a story-telling mood." He added that on the ranchos, where there was no telephone, very few books and very little excitement, "men like Jesus took the place of these diversions."[236] The description seems to be an apt one for Uncle Mike as well.

A true Californio, Uncle Mike lived at the adobe from 1880 until 1921, when he turned his apartment over to his relative Julia Murillo Coronado and her husband, Luis. However, Uncle Mike's presence continued to be felt years later. In 1966, the Rancho (by this time a historic site) hosted an open house for former tenants. The *Long Beach Independent Press Telegram* carried a story describing the event, which included music by the Long Beach Municipal Band. Some of the tenants had not returned to the site since the home had been remodeled in 1930. Many of the memories shared that evening centered on Uncle Mike and his tales. The article ended with the statement, "Presiding over it all seemed to be the spirit of one Miguel Murillo, the best doggoned vaquero in Southern California, the best storyteller and the best ghost anyone could hope to have haunt a house."

The Coronado and Liera Families in the 1920s

With the Bixby family no longer in residence at the adobe, very little in the way of upkeep was done to the building, particularly after Jotham's death in 1917. Photographs over the years document the deterioration of the walls, which were not protected with a yearly coat of whitewash. The north and south "work wings" of the adobe stood empty. The house had no electricity and no indoor plumbing; rather, a six-seat outhouse was located off the

Photograph of the Rancho adobe showing its deteriorating condition, with the outhouse to the right of the house, circa 1900–1920. *Courtesy of University of Southern California Libraries and California Historical Society.*

northeast corner of the house. There was no heating in the house. When it was cold, Concepción Coronado said, "We just went to bed, that's all. We would bundle up."

Luis and Julia Coronado paid ten dollars a month to rent the north end of the two-story house, while the Liera family paid the same amount for the rooms on the south end of the house. Luis Coronado's family was from Mexico, while Julia's parents, Lazaro Murillo and Agapita Mireles, were born in California in the 1850s. Luis worked first at Rancho Los Alamitos and then at the Virginia Country Club as a groundskeeper. The Virginia Country Club had been established in 1909 in what is today Recreation Park. The club moved to its present location, a stone's throw from the Rancho adobe, in 1921.

Mariano and Maria Liera heard from their friends the Coronados about lodging available at the Rancho. The Lieras were from Mexico, where their son Manuel was born. Mariano had owned some Holstein and Jersey cows when the family lived in Stanton, and he made his living selling boxes of homemade Mexican cheese and milk. The Lieras moved into the south half of the main house in 1921. Manuel moved in with them about a year later

Left: Agapita Mireles and Lazaro Murillo, parents of tenant Julia Murillo Coronado, circa 1890. *Rancho Los Cerritos Collection.*

Below: The Virginia Country Club (*right*) and Rancho Los Cerritos in 1928. *Rancho Los Cerritos Collection.*

and was hired as a groundskeeper at the golf course, where his pay was $2.80 a day. He described his work at the country club:

> *I came in 1922, and they were just starting the grounds, the fairways. I got to work on the fairways. It was a lot of hard 'dobe and we put in a lot of straw from the barnyard, kept the surface wet, and spread Bermuda seed to get those fairways established. I helped build some of the greens, and they gave me the job of watering the greens at night. I did it for sixteen years. I even did the underground sprinkler system.*

The Coronado children told stories of growing up at the Rancho, digging for coins hidden in the adobe walls of the house and playing down by the river. Concepción recalled, "There were trees, thick, willows. A few tules now and then. Watercress. And during that time, we had water in the river all year round. We'd take our lunch and we'd go in swimming in the water down there."

Her sister, Virginia, recalled an entrepreneurial venture the children engaged in:

> *There used to be that gate* [pointing to the courtyard gate]. *It used to swing out, and there would be people come here, and we'd charge them a quarter. We'd take them all through the house, and we'd tell them to be very quiet because the ghosts didn't like to be disturbed.* [Laughter] *So we made money off of them. All day there would be people coming here. We'd charge them to come in. Then my dad would come home and he'd find out what we pulled. Oh, he'd give us the devil.*

One of Concepción's jobs was getting water for the family. "As a child I got water with a big pail. That is how I met Manuel. I went to the Virginia Country Club for water with my pail and saw him working there." When the couple was courting, Concepción stated, "I loved dancing. We used to go to Long Beach and dance at the Silver Spray and the Cinderella on the Pike."

Manuel and Concepción were married in 1924 at St. Anthony's Church in Long Beach. Manuel recalled that about three or four dozen of the chickens he raised were slaughtered to provide food for the eighty guests who attended their wedding reception. Concepción added that the guests included "the Dominguez and the Cruz, Mr. and Mrs. Dominguez and one of the Figueroas: old-timers, pioneers. My mother knew them all."

Left: Manuel Liera and Concepción Coronado on their wedding day at RLC, 1924. *Rancho Los Cerritos Collection.*

Below: Tenant Manuel Liera with his chickens circa 1925. *Rancho Los Cerritos Collection.*

The wedding party was held in the large upstairs room that tenants referred to as Mr. Temple's *salón de baile*, or ballroom. There was dancing and music; the Coronado uncles played the violin, guitar and banjo. There was no electricity in the house, so the country club where Manuel worked strung a cord from the clubhouse next door to provide lights.

The couple's first child was born at the adobe. Concepción's recounting of Manuel delivering their first child at the ranch house illustrates their calm response in the face of difficulty:

> *Our daughter was born the 25th of April, 1926. She was our first child. Our doctor was a Polish doctor, Dr. Susdaski, and he lived in North Long Beach. We didn't have a phone and we had to depend on time and the ability to do the best we could until the doctor got here. Of course he came right away, as soon as I told him. He knew the place. But the baby came first, and she was there when he arrived.*

When asked by the interviewer if she had been afraid, Concepción answered categorically, "No, I wasn't afraid at all."

Although no repairs were made to the adobe by the owners during the time that the Coronados and Lieras lived there, Manuel did make a number of improvements himself. He built an outside wooden staircase on the south end of the veranda so that he could reach his chickens more easily. There was no kitchen upstairs on the south side of the house where the couple was living (in the former salón de baile). Manuel told an interviewer, "The room wasn't a kitchen. We made it into a kitchen. I built a sink. In fact, I still have the tools that I built it with." Concepción added, "I remember standing at the window, watching him come home from work." The families used the garden for planting corn, squash, carrots, lettuce, cabbage, green beans, peas and radishes.

Housing and Families

In 1906, the city council of Los Angeles created the Los Angeles City Housing Commission to address housing conditions in the city, specifically in house courts: rows of units, typically facing each other across an interior courtyard, with a thin wall separating each unit. Family dwellings within the house courts commonly consisted of two rooms: a kitchen and sleeping area. Tenants shared outside toilets located in the courtyard, and all water came from outdoor faucets. Historians Antonio Rios-Bustamante and Pedro Castillo stated, "According to Jacob Riis, who authored a classic study of living conditions among New York City's poor (*How the Other Half Lives*, 1890), housing conditions in Los Angeles were comparable to the worst tenements of Manhattan."[237]

Many of the court houses of Los Angeles were occupied by Mexican and Mexican American families. Rent for the homes ranged from $3.00 to $16.00 a month, at a time when the average laborer's salary was $1.85/day. The housing conditions of the Rancho adobe during the Tenant Era were similar to those documented by the Los Angeles Housing Commission survey of 1912. Families at the Rancho occupied one or two rooms, without electricity or indoor plumbing; bathroom facilities were an outhouse. At the same time, Concepción and Manuel Liera felt that the ten dollars a month they paid in rent was a fair price, given the advantage that the home was close to his place of work.

The young couple's living conditions exemplified the sharp differences between their life experiences and those of the members of the exclusive Virginia Country Club nearby. Concepción stated, "When I was a young girl, we didn't have any music." Manuel described a peanut tube radio that he constructed with plans from *Popular Mechanics* magazine: "I made this little radio, and it worked. We had a lot of fun with it. We had no other form of entertainment." However, they did hear music from the nearby country club. "From upstairs we could hear the music, especially when they had big parties. We could hear them laughing, and they had orchestras playing." They were also recruited occasionally to work at the club parties, serving coffee or working as a cigarette girl.

Tenant residents on the Rancho, like the Arias and Liera families, included immigrants from Mexico and their second-generation children. Other families, such as the Murillo and Cañedo families and the "pioneer" families who attended Concepción and Manuel's wedding, were Californios with roots in California dating to the 1830s. Early Long Beach resident Arthur Davies referred to them as "California Spanish. They weren't Mexican, because they'd never been to Mexico. But they had a Spanish name." Many of the Californio families had also intermarried with Indigenous people over the years. For example, Miguel Murillo was known as the Old Indian because of his Indigenous ancestors, and he too married an Indigenous woman.

Juanita Clara Murillo Cline, daughter of Miguel Murillo, at the Soboba Indian Reservation near Hemet, California, circa 1940. *Rancho Los Cerritos Collection.*

California historian George Phillips concluded his 1980 article titled "Indians in Los Angeles 1781–1875" with the statement: "In their descent into disappearance, they engaged in activity, both productive and destructive, that contributed significantly to the social and economic history of the pueblo's first century." Although Phillips highlighted economic contributions of the Indigenous people to the growth of Los Angeles, he also contributed to the myth that the Indigenous peoples had "disappeared" and their lives and experiences were relegated to the past.

Tenant recollections in the RLC archives document the continued presence of Indigenous people, which undoubtedly included the Tongva, in settlements and graveyards in early Long Beach. The Bustamante siblings, in their eighties when they were interviewed in 1966, recalled: "There's a graveyard on Long Beach Boulevard and American Avenue right on the corner, an old Indian graveyard. It's all covered up. They took up the little wood crosses." They also described settlements along the river:

> *A bunch of Indians used to live right below here where the apple orchard was, right down here by the driveway, out by the gate. Right straight down, they camped about halfway. Used to be the Indian settlement long time ago. They built that side made out of mud. On the other side of the river,* [there was] *another little Indian settlement further down.*

A Window into the Past

Most of the experiences recounted in this chapter are taken from oral history interviews carried out between the mid-1960s and the early 2000s by Rancho staff and volunteers (see bibliography). These interviews provide more firsthand accounts by numerous residents of the Rancho during the Tenant Era than would be available in published sources alone. Over one hundred interviews in the Rancho archives preserve memories of Bixby family members, tenants who lived at the adobe or farmed on Rancho lands and residents of early Long Beach. One of the tenants, Frank Coronado, reflected on the importance of preserving these oral histories:

> *When I retire, I would like to write a book about the things I know. I would remember a lot because those things die. You have to have somebody start that ember that still burns a little bit—start it up again—and you start remembering those things.*

CHAPTER 7

FROM PRIVATE RESIDENCE TO HISTORIC SITE

Long Beach is several towns in one—a seaside resort, a haven for elderly retired persons, and an industrial center drawing its income from oil, shipping, and manufacturing. Its population is correspondingly diverse—including amusement zone barkers, sailors and Naval officers and their families, oil and factory workers, retired farmers and tradesmen from the Middle West.[238]

—California in the 1930s: The WPA Guide to the Golden State

This description of Long Beach is taken from a guidebook to California written by anonymous authors of the Federal Writers Project and published in 1939. The Federal Writers Project was part of the Works Progress Administration, one of the New Deal initiatives designed to fight the Depression by providing work for those who were unemployed. In California, more than one-quarter of the state's workers were unemployed, and crowds joined "hunger marches" in protest.[239]

At the onset of the Great Depression following the stock market crash of 1929, most of the land that had formed Rancho Los Cerritos had been sold for the establishment of Long Beach and surrounding cities. One of the remaining plots was the 4.7-acre site that included the old adobe home, which stood empty at the time. This final chapter documents developments spanning from the 1930s to the present day: the remodeling of the adobe by Llewellyn Bixby Sr. as his private residence, the changes across former Rancho lands and the preservation of RLC as a historic site.

Llewellyn Bixby Sr. and Avis Bixby

Llewellyn Bixby Sr. (1879–1942) purchased the Rancho Los Cerritos adobe in 1930 from the Jotham Bixby Company with the intent to refurbish and remodel the house, which had been allowed to fall into disrepair during tenant occupancy. Llewellyn Sr. was the son of Jotham Bixby's older brother, Lewellyn, and his wife, Mary Hathaway Bixby. Lewellyn had been a founding partner in Flint, Bixby & Co. and had first come to California during the gold rush.

A word should be said about the Bixby family Llewellyns. *Lewellyn*, with a single initial letter *L*, was the original spelling of the name by the Bixby family in Maine. However, Lewellyn's son began writing his name with an initial *Ll*, the traditional Welsh spelling.[240] As the first family member with the *Ll* spelling, he became known as Llewellyn Sr., and his son became Llewellyn Bixby Jr.

Llewellyn Sr. was the younger brother of Sarah Bixby Smith, author of *Adobe Days*. The siblings grew up in the fashionable Bunker Hill neighborhood in Los Angeles, where their father managed the Southern California enterprises of Flint, Bixby & Co. Their mother, Mary Hathaway Bixby, passed away when Llewellyn was three years old, and he and his sisters were raised by their aunt, Martha Hathaway. Llewellyn spent time during summer vacations at Rancho Los Cerritos and on Catalina Island.

Llewellyn finished his last two years of high school at the preparatory school associated with Pomona College, and there he met his future wife, Lilian Avis Bixby. They both enrolled in Pomona College, where Llewellyn played on the football team.

Opposite, top: Avis Smith Bixby circa 1915. *Rancho Los Cerritos Collection.*

Opposite, bottom: Llewellyn Bixby Sr. circa 1928. *Rancho Los Cerritos Collection.*

Right: Llewellyn Bixby Sr. and his wife, Avis Bixby, onboard ship on their cruise to Europe in 1904. *Rancho Los Cerritos Collection.*

Llewellyn and Avis (her preferred name) graduated in 1901 and married soon afterward, becoming the first of four generations of Bixby family members to meet at Pomona College and marry.[241] They moved to Boston, where Llewellyn studied civil engineering at the Massachusetts Institute of Technology for two years. After a trip to Europe in 1904, the couple returned to Los Angeles and later Long Beach.

Llewellyn entered the family businesses, joining the Bixby Land Company in 1905 and the board of the Alamitos Land Company in 1907.[242] Llewellyn never worked as a civil engineer; however, he did do some surveying as part of his work for the Bixby companies. His son, Llewellyn Jr., remembered serving as his "rod man" when his father surveyed the Virginia Country Club location. He described the rod man as "the guy that held the stick that went way out ahead, and Father followed along behind with his transit on a tripod."

As a child, Llewellyn Jr. had occasion to visit his father's office in Long Beach. He enjoyed swinging on the waist-high gates that led to separate little offices. He remembered details such as his father's big rolltop desk and the bookkeeper who sat on a high stool in the corner. "He would dip his pen in an inkwell and did all hand entries of bookkeeping in great big ledgers."

In 1921, Llewellyn Sr. became president of the Bixby Land Company and remained president until his death in 1942. He was also vice president of the Alamitos Land Company, treasurer of the Los Angeles Dock and Terminal Company and president of several other Bixby family operations, such as the Soft Water Laundry Company and the Long Beach Dairy and Creamery.[243]

In addition to his involvement in family businesses, Llewellyn was one of the original financiers of Balboa Amusement Producing Company (between Sixth and Seventh Streets on Alamitos Avenue), where silent movies were filmed. Long Beach was an early site of the motion picture business, and Balboa Studios, known as the world's most productive and innovative silent film studio, was home to stars such as Buster Keaton and Fatty Arbuckle. The location is the current site of the Museum of Latin American Art (MOLA).

Llewellyn and Avis loved to travel and took their young children on automobile trips across country, to Maine in 1915 and to Arizona, New Mexico and Colorado in 1917. In 1918 they visited Zion and Yellowstone National Parks, and several summers were spent at Yosemite National Park. Avis and the children stayed in Yosemite Valley, while Llewellyn, an avid hiker, joined the Sierra Club on its annual "high trip" hikes into the backcountry of the park. In 1929, just months before the stock market crash, Llewellyn and Avis set out on a long-postponed trip around the world, which took them to Singapore, Cambodia, Bombay, Alexandria, Greece and Naples.

REMODELING OF THE ADOBE

As early as 1913, Jotham Bixby and his son George had expressed interest in restoring the old adobe Rancho home. Although structurally sound, the house required reroofing, repair and modernization. An article in the *Long Beach Press Telegram* in January 1913 described their plans to restore it to "as far as practicable, the style and atmosphere of the past."[244] Restoration plans did not come to fruition until years later, when Jotham's nephew Llewellyn Sr. expressed an interest in purchasing the family property. He was offered the opportunity to purchase the adobe and surrounding four acres of land, located beside the Virginia Country Club where he played golf, for just one dollar.

Architect Kenneth Wing was hired to design the renovation project. He combined the original Monterey Colonial style of the house with the Mission

Virginia Country Club circa 1926. *Rancho Los Cerritos Collection.*

Revival style that had become popular in California in the early part of the twentieth century.[245] This style was inspired by the "Spanish colonial mission heritage" of California and was characterized by elements such as thick white stucco walls, red tile roofs and deep window and door openings. In the case of the Rancho adobe, the original home was an authentic product of the Mexican period of California history. The Mission Revival style, however, exemplified a movement in architecture and popular culture that celebrated a romanticized view of history that recast California settlement as primarily "Spanish" while ignoring Mexican contributions. As historian Chelsea Vaughn explains, "Proponents of this fantasy past imagined a regional history populated by lovely señoritas and regular fiestas."[246]

Renovation work was carried out by the construction firm of C.T. McGrew and Sons. The decision was made to retain the shape and walls of the old adobe as much as possible, with newly constructed doors and hardware based on original styles. This involved, for example, retaining the uneven, undulating surfaces of the adobe walls and saving one of the windowsills that was marked by the teeth of a horse that had been tethered there during the sheep ranch period. Changes to the original adobe included the addition of a sunporch and a red tile roof and the removal of a ceiling

The Rancho courtyard during the remodel, 1930. *Rancho Los Cerritos Collection.*

The newly renovated courtyard. *Rancho Los Cerritos Collection.*

to create a spacious, high-ceilinged living room. In the single-story wings, walls were removed or altered to create bedrooms, bathrooms, a four-car garage and servants' quarters. Renovations also included upgrades such as gas furnaces, indoor plumbing and electricity.

It was during reconstruction that the eleven cogged stones dating from 6750 BCE were unearthed. These stones were displayed by Llewellyn Sr.'s family in one of their curio cabinets and currently form part of the RLC museum collections. The renovation project also included earthquake retrofitting, which was fortuitous given the Long Beach earthquake of 1933 that caused destruction throughout the city. The Rancho adobe survived the earthquake without damage.

The decorative gardens, with their formal beds, that had been John Temple's pride and joy had largely disappeared by 1930. During the Tenant Era, the gardens had been used for other purposes, including the raising of chickens, planting of corn and vegetables and even the cultivation of tobacco. Llewellyn Sr. engaged Ralph Cornell, a well-known landscape designer, to redesign the gardens in keeping with the newly renovated home. The garden featured a sweeping driveway entrance to the home and a central curving lawn surrounding the majestic Moreton Bay fig tree that had been planted by the Jotham Bixby family. The inner courtyard, no longer the dirt courtyard of the cattle and sheep ranching days, now featured a brick terrace and walkways as well as a reflecting pool in the center.

Family Life During the Great Depression

Llewellyn Sr. and Avis moved into their newly renovated home on St. Patrick's Day 1931. After graduating from Pomona College in 1930, their son Llewellyn Jr. went on a trip around the world with two friends. He returned to live with his parents at the Rancho until his marriage to Betty (Elizabeth) in 1934.

When Llewellyn Jr. returned to Long Beach, he recalled realizing "the straits the family was in." He went on to observe:

> *The depression had hit them an awful blow because they were land poor. Bixby Land Co. had 4,500 acres that ran from Signal Hill to Los Alamitos and nothing much to grow on it and no way of doing anything except paying taxes.*

Paul Dudley Jr. (the son of Avis and Llewellyn's daughter Avis and her husband, Paul Dudley) offered his reflections on how his family experienced the Depression. As a child, he remembered coming out to the Rancho for Sunday dinners with his grandparents during the 1930s.

> *These were hard times, and I didn't realize until far later that Grandmother and Granddad, Papa and Granny, were quite well off, even though he had suffered quite some reversals in the early thirties. What we had there was a cook and a maid. And roast beef, leg of lamb—those type of things—were the two standard things* [served].

The 1940 census lists the three resident workers at the Rancho, including the groundskeeper Arthur Orchard; the maid Marie Getinasso, aged thirty-one; and the cook Lydia Hughes, aged fifty-six. Family records indicate that the women worked sixty hours a week. There was also a Chinese man who came and did laundry for the family. Paul Jr. described the wired bell system in the house that was used to summon various staff members. He recalled "that fascinating thing to me as a young boy, the thing that Granny would step on and summon someone to come in and do something, a buzzer—just wonderful." He would crawl under the table to play with it.

In discussing the styles and purposes of the different rooms in the house, Paul Jr. remarked about the living room that "the formal room back here with the piano…was musty and dusty, with a kind of brownish carpet. [It] was not particularly well lit, not a room that had any great character until Christmas and Thanksgiving, the holidays." By contrast, he described the current library as the "hub" of the house where everyone liked to gather: "The light would stick in this room. This is where the puzzles were put together, conversations, with three or four people reading, the books were around you; this was the hub." A cabinet in the upstairs hallway held shells, travel souvenirs and golf trophies (Llewellyn Sr. was a left-handed champion at Virginia Country Club).

Paul's father and grandfather shared an interest in photography, and Llewellyn Sr. had a darkroom in one of the rooms along the south wing of the house. The RLC archives include numerous photographs of the grandchildren and family members in the gardens, but only one photograph survives of the interior of the house. It shows the furnishing of the sunporch that was added as part of the remodeling.

Left: Stephen and Paul Dudley, grandsons of Llewellyn Bixby Sr., in the Rancho gardens. *Rancho Los Cerritos Collection.*

Below: The sunporch added to the adobe home as part of the remodel. *Rancho Los Cerritos Collection.*

ARTHUR ORCHARD

Arthur Orchard was the best known of the Rancho staff during the period of family residence beginning in 1931 to the time that the property was sold to the city in 1955. He lived in the north wing past the kitchen and kept the cars serviced, took care of the yard and did general maintenance. His parents had immigrated from England and settled in New Jersey. Due to health issues, Arthur moved to the drier climate of California. He was fondly remembered by Paul Dudley's younger brother Stephen, who described him as a "substitute grandfather."

Stephen enjoyed spending time with Arthur and helping with the gardening. An early example of his "helping" was fixing a little wagon behind an old, powerful, very heavy lawnmower and making it a "riding mower."

After his family moved out of the adobe, Stephen would often say to them, "I'm going over to Arthur's" and would ride his bike over on Saturdays to help with mowing lawns and raking leaves.

> *Some of the fun things were our big bonfires periodically where we'd have to burn the debris. We'd either burn out where the Visitor Center is now or out the gates from behind the lawn and go down towards the country club there on the back side. We kept two big piles. When the piles got too big, we'd set them on fire on a foggy morning…* [Then] *we would put potatoes in the ashes and let them cook while we were doing our fire, and then usually in the afternoon we'd have a wonderful potato snack.*

After the Rancho became a museum, the family retired Arthur and continued to pay his salary. Stephen shared, "He wasn't paid that much, but it was more than enough for him, and we just kept on paying him. He found a little apartment nearby, because it was right by the Los Cerritos Market and easy for him to live there." After his retirement, the family continued to invite Arthur over for dinner fairly frequently.

Opposite: Arthur Orchard standing in front of the Moreton Bay fig tree circa 1947. *Rancho Los Cerritos Collection.*

Above: Arthur Orchard and Stephen Dudley working in the garden in 1942. *Rancho Los Cerritos Collection.*

Developments on Former Rancho Lands During the Depression

The population of Long Beach was changing, no longer characterized by the numerous retirees from the Midwest who had made the town their home in the early part of the century. Many African Americans moved to the Los Angeles and Long Beach area as part of what is known as the Great Migration—when, beginning in around 1910, over six million African Americans moved out of the rural southern United States to the urban

Northeast, Midwest and West Coast, seeking refuge from segregation and violence. However, they encountered racism and discrimination on the West Coast as well. The Ku Klux Klan had emerged as a powerful force in Long Beach, holding rallies and events throughout the 1920s. In a parade in 1926, thirty thousand Klansmen marched from Bixby Park down Ocean Boulevard.[247] The 1930s saw increasing white resistance to the efforts of Black residents to secure rental and housing ownership in Long Beach.

African American residents as well as families of former Rancho farm and dairy workers living in Long Beach were affected by redlining practices that established limitations on the neighborhoods in which they could purchase homes. The official website of the City of Long Beach features a "Timeline of Racial Inequities in Long Beach" that includes a description of the redlining and racial covenants that were common in this period:

> *In 1934 the Federal Housing Association and private banks implemented redlining, which restricted loans based on the racial makeup of the neighborhood. Central Long Beach—where many people of color lived—was a redlined neighborhood, deemed too risky for investment by lenders. During this same time, deed restrictions prohibited the purchase, lease, or occupation of property by anybody who wasn't white. These restrictions were common in parts of East Long Beach, Bixby Knolls, and Lakewood.*

Beginning in 1931, families of Mexican descent were caught up in the repatriation of Mexican nationals and people of Mexican descent. Officials, worried that welfare rolls would be unduly strained, supported the rounding up and deportation of Mexicans. The American Federation of Labor (AFL) supported widespread deportation of Mexicans based on the assumption that more jobs would be available for "deserving Americans" as a result.[248] Immigration agents went door to door in ethnic neighborhoods, demanding that residents provide proof of citizenship or risk incarceration. People were offered the option to "voluntarily" return to Mexico or else face a deportation process that would involve being put on buses or trains and sent across the border to Mexico.[249]

Hortencia Zavala Nieto was a Long Beach resident whose father, facing the threat of deportation, decided to return to Mexico. He brought his five children, all of whom were born in the United States, to live with his parents there. Hortencia recalled being forced to work in the fields as a young child. A U.S. citizen, she longed to return to California but was unable to do so until 1944.[250] Repatriation occurred across many different states, and an estimated seventy-five thousand people were forced from Southern California to Mexico during the 1930s. An estimated 60 percent of those deported were U.S. citizens—many of them, like Hortencia, "repatriated" to a country in which they had never resided.

World War II Years

The entrance of the United States into World War II marked the end of the Great Depression.[251] Long Beach, with its growing harbor facility and strategic location on the West Coast, was on high alert for air attacks. A *Long Beach Press Telegram* ad at the time cautioned residents, "Military authorities have repeatedly warned that enemy aerial attacks on this vital defense area are both possible and probable."[252]

Construction of the Terminal Island Naval Dry Docks had been authorized in 1940 and began with one large dry dock and two smaller docks. During World War II, the naval dry docks expanded and provided repairs to tankers, cargo ships, troop transports, destroyers and cruisers. By the end of the war, over sixteen thousand civilians were employed at the facility.

Following the attack on Pearl Harbor on December 7, 1941, there was rampant fear on the part of West Coast residents of possible sabotage or espionage by people of Japanese descent. The day after the bombing, 300 Japanese residents of Long Beach were detained. Although the director of the FBI, J. Edgar Hoover, reported that there was no evidence of Japanese Americans providing support to the enemy, plans proceeded for the removal of "any and all persons considered a threat to national security."[253] In February 1942, after California attorney general Earl Warren ordered the removal of Japanese residents, President Franklin Roosevelt signed Executive Order 9066, which resulted in the incarceration of 120,000 Japanese Americans for the duration of the war. Japanese Americans, both first-generation issei and second-generation nisei, were forcibly relocated to internment camps in remote areas in the western United States. Many from the Los Angeles area were sent to the Manzanar camp in the Owens Valley. Over half of those incarcerated were U.S. citizens.

In Long Beach, Japanese residents of Terminal Island were forced to leave behind businesses they had built over generations. Tenant farmers on Alamitos Land Company property had to leave their farms and equipment. Llewellyn Bixby Jr. reported that although other tenants were found to take

Families of Japanese ancestry, with their belongings, await a train to take them to the Merced Assembly Center. *Courtesy of War Relocation Authority photographs: Japanese-American evacuation and resettlement, WRA No. C-492, the Bancroft Library, University of California, Berkeley.*

over the farms left behind by the Japanese families, these tenants "took advantage of them [and] bought their equipment at unconscionable prices." The Japanese Presbyterian Church on Locust Avenue, constructed in 1925, was taken over by the Long Beach Boys Club. Members of the congregation were forced to spend several years after they returned from internment camps pressuring the club to relinquish the building.[254]

Avis and Llewellyn Bixby Sr. were in residence at the Rancho after the outbreak of the war; however, Llewellyn suffered a heart attack and died in 1942. His son, who had gotten his broker's license and was in the real estate business on his own, was recruited to return to the family business. Llewellyn Jr. recalled that George Bixby's widow, Amelia, called him up and said, "'Llewellyn, you come down and go to work.' She just sort of grabbed me by the scruff of the neck and said, 'You go to work for the companies.'" He recalled that among his tasks for the Jotham Bixby Company was subdividing the Bixby Knolls neighborhood.

After her husband's death in 1942, Avis Bixby continued to live on her own in the large home for a few years before moving to the Villa Riviera apartments in downtown Long Beach. In an interview carried out with the RLC museum curator in 2002, Avis's granddaughters Barbara Bixby Blackwell and Jean Bixby Smith shared memories of their grandmother. Jean noted that Avis was particularly known for her love of travel.

> *The story I remember was the time that she called up Dad and said, "Llewellyn, the* Caronia *is here." And Dad said, "Okay, why didn't you tell me it was coming in?" She said, "Well, I want to know where it's going. I might want to go." So she called up and found out where it was going and decided she wanted to go. But she couldn't get herself ready in time because it was sailing the next day. It was going to San Francisco, so she packed her bags and got her ticket and flew to San Francisco and got on the* Caronia, *which was one of her favorite ships.*

Jean described her grandmother as a "very strong-willed woman." She was very strict about not serving alcohol at home or even attending parties at which alcohol was served. Jotham and Margaret Bixby, in the generation previous, were also "very much on the dry side of things, and they put alcohol restrictions in the deeds and the property they sold in downtown Long Beach." However, when Avis turned eighty, she surprised the family by hosting a cocktail party—"where everybody else will have more fun"—for her birthday celebration.

Avis's grandson Stephen described going to pick her up to take her to Llewellyn's for Thanksgiving and Christmas gatherings. Later, he recounted going to pick up his grandmother in his 1924 Model-T.

> *We told grandmother, "Steve will be by to pick you up," and so I came by in the Model T,* [laughs] *picked her up, and she didn't bat an eye. She climbed right in, and down we went* [laughs]. *Everybody was very surprised at that.*

After Avis moved out of the old adobe, her daughter and son-in-law lived in the house for a brief period. During this time, their young son Stephen Dudley attended first grade at Cerritos School. His bedroom was in what was called "Llewellyn's room," which has since been refitted as the historic site's blacksmith shop. Stephen recalled being driven to school by his friend and Rancho groundskeeper Arthur Orchard in Arthur's Model A Ford. He also described playing with the surveyor's transit that had been used by his uncle and grandfather. "They were always dealing with real estate matters, and it was a very nice old brass transit on a tripod. So I would set that up in the yard and survey."

After the Dudley family moved out in 1947, the house remained unoccupied for several years. Stephen described having occasional problems with teenagers driving out to the site to party late at night. He claimed that the place was known as a haunted house, so it had a certain allure for young people.

> *We had two or three interesting times where my father...slept out in the orchard and I slept in the library. Occasionally he corralled a carload of kids, and so my job was to go wake Arthur and we'd call the police. My uncle knew the police chief, I guess, and they would sometimes come up here and park.*

With family no longer in permanent residence, and with the economic burden of keeping up the property, the decision was made to sell the Rancho property to the city. In addition, Arthur Orchard was reaching retirement age, and it was becoming more difficult for him to maintain the house and grounds. In December 1954, the property was leased to the city for one year for $10,000, with the agreement that this sum would be applied to the purchase price. The following year, the city exercised the option to buy the site for $80,000, and Rancho Los Cerritos opened to the public as a museum.

Stephen recalled the decision to sell to the city being a fairly easy one but described discussions regarding the bigger decision of how the home would be interpreted. Questions addressed included:

> *What do we really want to do with the house? Do we consider it as a house that has been restored as it is and utilize that but also talk about the earlier history? Or do we unrestore it and take it back to 1844?*

Once the decision was made to keep the house in its current condition, as opposed to how it looked in 1870, figuring out programming became easier. This decision continues to affect the interpretation of the site for museum visitors today.

Continued Bixby Family Involvement in Long Beach

Long Beach residents are familiar with the many properties in the city that bear the Bixby name and attest to the family's prominence in local history. Bixby Elementary School, Bixby Road, Bixby Knolls, Bixby Towers and Bixby Park are among the many locales bearing the family name. In a lengthy interview carried out in 1984, Llewellyn Bixby Jr. recounted his service with other family members on the boards of various family enterprises, stating that stock ownership in the Bixby Land Company was "closely held.... Everybody sort of hangs together." He described Bixby Land Company ownership of stock as "still 99 percent in the hands of lineal descendants."

Llewellyn Jr. did not know John Bixby, who had passed away in 1887, but he worked with John's daughter Susanna when they served on the Alamitos Land Company board of directors together in the 1940s. Amelia Bixby became a close friend. "After I came down with the company, she was my right arm when I needed somebody to lean on in the company."

Llewellyn Jr. enjoyed a friendly, informal relationship with John's son Fred. Fred Bixby was the president of Alamitos Land Company, and Llewellyn used to call on Fred at Rancho Los Alamitos on company projects. Fred had "quite a stock of bonded whiskey that he'd laid in in Prohibition that seemed to be bottomless. [We'd] sit around and have a nip and talk things over." He fondly remembered Fred as a great raconteur, particularly of cowboy stories.

In addition to serving on the boards of multiple family enterprises, Llewellyn Jr. was appointed to the Long Beach Board of Harbor Commissioners in 1965 and served until 1977. In his twelve years on the board, he saw the Long Beach harbor move into containerization, or the use of standard-sized containers to move freight. Because Long Beach was a new, man-made harbor, it could more easily convert to containerization than, for example, the Los Angeles port with its older warehouses and facilities. Llewellyn resigned from the board when "they came up with this new law that you had to reveal all your assets."

Outside of the businesses, the Bixbys were involved in community service, particularly in the area of education. Llewellyn Jr.'s wife, Betty, and Fred's wife, Florence, were long-serving founding members of the Long Beach Day Nursery, founded in 1912.[255] The nursery was one of the first licensed childcare programs in California, the first licensed program in Long Beach and the first to meet the accreditation standards of the National Association for the Education of Young Children. Betty was on the board for nineteen years, until a term limit law was passed, and she and her daughter Jean each served as president. Betty added that it was "quite an institution because it had so many of the old Long Beach people on it to begin with."

The family was also quite involved with the Claremont colleges. Sarah Hathaway Bixby donated the land for Scripps College and was a founding trustee. Later, Jean Bixby Smith served as chairman of the board of Scripps College. George Bixby was a Pomona trustee, and Susannah Bixby Bryant was the first female trustee. She was also the founder of the Rancho Santa Ana Botanic Garden in Claremont, California, the largest botanic garden in the state that houses California native plants. Llewellyn Bixby Sr. was also a trustee of Pomona from 1909 to 1942. Martha Hathaway was a major supporter of Pomona, and her 1903 house is now the home of the president of Claremont McKenna College.

RANCHO EQUESTRIAN LEGACY

Just as members of the Bixby family, past Rancho owners, continue to form part of the fabric of Long Beach, former Rancho workers and tenants also participate in and contribute to city life. The experiences of the Bixby family, with generational interconnections from the sheep ranching period through the present, are mirrored by those of the Valenzuela family as recorded in an article in the *Long Beach Press Telegram* in April 1993. Alfred Valenzuela's grandfather, originally from Chile, worked as a sheepherder for the Bixby family on one of their ranchos in the San Luis Obispo area before coming to work at Rancho Los Cerritos. His son Paul followed in his footsteps, working as a vaquero and sheepherder for George Bixby and later for Fred Bixby of Rancho Los Alamitos. By the time his son Alfred was born, Paul was working as a beet farmer as well as raising horses and clearing land with his horse-drawn rig. He was asked by Earl Daugherty to clear land for his airfield, which later became the first site of the Long Beach Municipal Airport.

In the 1920s, Fred Bixby rewarded Paul's service over the years with the gift of an acre of land on a hill near Rancho Los Cerritos along Golden Avenue. As a child, Alfred attended Cerritos School, which still stands on Willow Street east of Santa Fe Avenue. However, he left school at age fourteen to work as a ranch hand at Rancho Las Margaritas, breaking horses and driving cattle. He met and married Adela Olivares, the daughter of the Las Margaritas foreman. After their marriage, the couple returned to the family home in Long Beach, where Alfred worked as a milker while he continued to raise horses and participate in rodeos and competitions.

The Valenzuelas maintained their rural lifestyle until 1966, when their homestead in an unincorporated part of Los Angeles County became part of Long Beach. The Valenzuela home was subsequently condemned by city inspectors as an illegally converted barn. Alfred responded by tearing down the building and constructing a new home on the property. By the 1980s, despite the Valenzuelas' claim that their property predated any other homes in the Wrigley Heights neighborhood, the area was rezoned by the city and their animals were banished. Alfred and Adela continued to live in their home as lots were sold and homes built around them, and Alfred continued to care for his herd of five horses, housed in a rented stable.

Currently, and perhaps ironically, the city permits the raising of horses in equestrian-zoned lots facing Golden Avenue just to the south of the area where the Valenzuela home was located. Horse paddocks are found along the Wrigley Greenbelt, located on Los Angeles River flood control land between Willow Street and Thirty-Fourth Street.[256] The greenbelt includes a one-mile walking trail amid landscaping of drought-resistant native plants. A recent article in the *Los Angeles Times* describes the still-vibrant vaquero community in the area. Each Sunday night, local *charros* (Mexican cowboys) meet in a downtown parking lot to demonstrate their equestrian skills and champion horses in "El Show de los Caballos."

Tongva Today

Rancho Los Cerritos is located on the ancestral and current homelands of the Tongva people. The Rancho's land acknowledgement statement honors and extends respect to the Gabrielino/Tongva people as the past, present and future caretakers of the Los Angeles Basin and Southern Channel Island lands. At the time of the 2010 census, close to 2,500 people in California self-identified as Tongva. Despite numerous attempts at assimilation and removal, the Tongva never left their ancestral lands. They are still here, playing an active part in the Southern California community.

In 1994, the State of California officially recognized the Gabrielino-Tongva Tribe as the "aboriginal tribe of the Los Angeles Basin." The Tongva continue to lobby for recognition at the federal level, however. Fulfilling Bureau of Indian Affairs requirements for federal recognition is particularly onerous for unrecognized California tribes due to the devastation suffered within the Franciscan missions.[257]

Tongva people currently work to save landmarks of cultural importance and to educate the public about their history and culture. One of the Tongva efforts to revive and preserve their cultural heritage is exemplified by the activities of the Ti'at Society. Tongva descendant Cindi Alvitre, cofounder of the Ti'at Society and professor of American Indian studies at California State University, Long Beach, said she was inspired by a vision to establish the society and collaborate with Indigenous boatbuilders to construct a full-size oceangoing vessel.[258] In 1995, the society's ti'at *Moomat Ahiko* (*Breath of the Sea*) made its maiden voyage as the first ti'at known to have been built since the 1800s.

The Tongva Taraxat Paxaavxa Conservancy, a Tongva-led nonprofit whose name roughly translates to "The People's Land," was established with the purpose of stewarding the lands of Tovaangar. The conservancy's mission includes managing land back efforts to return control of ancestral lands to their original stewards and building community for Native people. With support from the First Nations' California Tribal Fund, an acre of property located at the base of the San Gabriel Mountains was repatriated to Taraxat Paxaavxa, who will use it to provide emergency housing and to grow and process Native foods. Conservancy vice president Kimberly Morales Johnson stated, "As a non–federally recognized tribe, this is our first chance to make history and to exercise self-determination and sovereignty, despite not having federal recognition."[259]

Rancho Los Cerritos in the Community

Rancho Los Cerritos was purchased by the City of Long Beach in 1955 and opened to the public as a museum. It has the distinction of being listed as a local, state and national historic landmark. The Rancho is not only a site that interprets that past; it also plays a vital role in the community and ongoing local history.

A key goal of the Rancho Los Cerritos Foundation is to expand access to the site and its history to all communities. Currently, the city has a population of close to 450,000 residents. Long Beach is one of the most ethnically and culturally diverse big cities in the United States, as recognized by the U.S. Census. According to 2020 census figures, the demographic makeup of the

Current view of the RLC courtyard. *Rancho Los Cerritos Collection.*

city was 43 percent Latino, 26 percent non-Hispanic White, 13 percent Asian, 12 percent African American and 2 percent Native American. The Rancho's vision is that all visitors will see themselves represented in Rancho programs and interpretation.

An integral part of RLC's mission to "honor diverse perspectives, enrich collaborative conversations, and inspire broader understanding through stewardship of Rancho Los Cerritos' natural and cultural history" is embodied in educational experiences for local schoolchildren. Fourth grade classes participate in the Adelante field trip experience, in which costumed docents portray Temple and Bixby family members and workers from the cattle and sheep ranching periods of Rancho history who are brought forward in time—*adelante*. The historical characters interact with students as they tour the house and native garden, examine historical artifacts and engage in nineteenth-century chores.

As part of its vision and mission, the Rancho partners with numerous community organizations on a variety of projects and events that foster collaboration and enhance experiences for all groups. One example of mutually beneficial collaboration takes place with Taking the Reins and Urban Saddles, nonprofit organizations that work with underserved youth in local communities. These organizations collaborated with RLC on

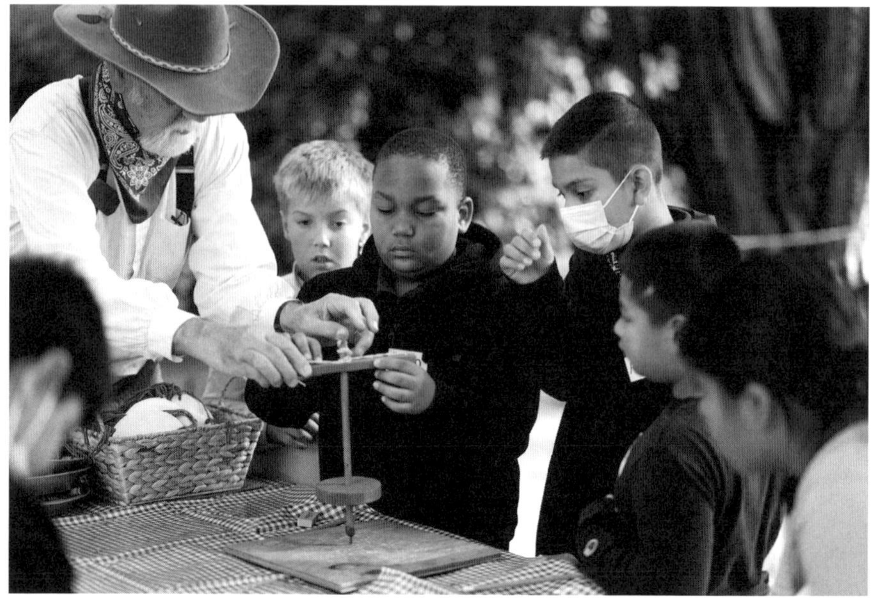

A volunteer docent works with fourth-grade students as part of the Adelante program, 2024. *Rancho Los Cerritos Collection.*

the *Untold Legacies: Rethinking the American Cowboy* exhibition and series of related events. Rooted in the rural experience of many African Americans who came to the Los Angeles area as part of the Great Migration, Urban Saddles provides opportunities for young people in Compton, Paramount and surrounding cities to develop confidence, riding skills, and experience in caring for animals. The organization's goals include the building of resilience and hope in local communities through the equine experience and the cowboy code of the West.

The Rancho is also committed to the environment and supports education around water conservation, climate change and environmental justice. As part of this commitment, the Port of Long Beach and the San Gabriel and Lower Los Angeles Rivers and Mountains Conservancy (RMC) are among the many donors supporting RLC interpretive programs for this type of work. In 2018, Rancho Los Cerritos was awarded a grant from the Port of Long Beach for a multifaceted water conservation program called Looking Back to Advance Forward. This funding permitted the construction of a drainage system featuring sustainable practices such as permeable surfaces, water basins, rain gardens and filter strips. By strategically reclaiming rainwater, the Rancho has the capacity to withstand large storms without damaging its historic landscapes. The water conservation design also uses traditional water-capturing techniques. Water flows to the Arroyo, the lowest point on the Rancho's property, where it naturally infiltrates the ground. Water treated through biofiltration recharges the aquifer.

The Rancho gardens feature elements from the 1930s renovation, such as a wisteria arbor and a side orchard. More recent additions include the Native Garden along the Arroyo, where plants native to Southern California are grown and where interpretation focuses on Tongva ecological knowledge, plant use and conservation. Volunteers and visitors to the gardens have the opportunity to participate each year in the four-day City Nature Challenge, in which participants use cameras to document all the wildlife observed at the Rancho. These findings are used by scientists who track biodiversity in the region.

The Rancho offers a variety of activities designed to share the site's rich history with the over fifteen thousand visitors who come each year. These activities are made possible through the work of a dedicated group of trained volunteer docents, greeters, garden assistants and crafts makers. Information about tours, exhibitions and programs can be found on the Rancho website: https://www.rancholoscerritos.org

Current view of the RLC gardens. *Rancho Los Cerritos Collection.*

Today, Rancho Los Cerritos Historic Site is a nonprofit museum and an integral part of the Long Beach community. Owned by the City of Long Beach, the site is governed by the Rancho Los Cerritos Foundation, which works to preserve the historic site and to honor and illuminate the region's cultural heritage through innovative opportunities that expand access to all communities. *Rancho Los Cerritos: People Who Shaped the Land* represents one contribution to the mission and vision of the site. It is our hope that readers will be inspired to visit and become involved with Rancho Los Cerritos.

NOTES

Chapter 1

1. Sarris, "Fidel's Place," 16.
2. Ramirez and Small, "Saging the World," 114.
3. Crespi and Piette, "Diary of Fray Juan Crespi," 376.
4. Reid, *Indians of Los Angeles County*, letter no. 17.
5. Madley, *American Genocide*, 16.
6. Lake, *Colonial Rosary*, 9; Madley, *American Genocide*, 3.
7. Madley, *American Genocide*, 23.
8. Anderson, *Tending the Wild*, 13.
9. Anderson, *Tending the Wild*, 57.
10. McCawley, *First Angelinos*, 2.
11. Koerper et al., "Cogged Stone Ritual Behavior," 121.
12. McCawley, *First Angelinos*, 9–10.
13. "Gabrielino/Tongva Nation," https://gabrielinotongva.org.
14. Greene and Curwen, "Tongva Villages."
15. McCawley, *First Angelinos*, 29.
16. McCawley, *First Angelinos*, 28.
17. Engstrand, *Rancho Los Cerritos*, 5.
18. Madley, *American Genocide*, 23.
19. B. Miller, *Gabrielino*, 106.
20. B. Miller, *Gabrielino*, 106.
21. McCawley, *First Angelinos*, 101.

22. McCawley, *First Angelinos*, 149.
23. McCawley, *First Angelinos*, 162–63.
24. Hewes and Hewes, "Indian Life and Customs," 93.
25. Anderson, *Tending the Wild*, 1.
26. Anderson, *Tending the Wild*, 3.
27. B. Miller, *Gabrielino*, 77.
28. B. Miller, *Gabrielino*, 78.
29. Anderson, *Tending the Wild*, 146.
30. B. Miller, *Gabrielino*, 77.
31. Heizer and Whipple, *California Indians*, 302.
32. B. Miller, *Gabrielino*, 47–48.
33. B. Miller, *Gabrielino*, 48.
34. B. Miller, *Gabrielino*, 77.
35. B. Miller, *Gabrielino*, 72.
36. B. Miller, *Gabrielino*, 70.
37. B. Miller, *Gabrielino*, 59.
38. B. Miller, *Gabrielino*, 93.
39. Engstrand, *Rancho Los Cerritos*, 4; Heizer and Whipple, *California Indians*, 44, 48.
40. Hyslop, *Contest for California*, 49–51.
41. Crespi and Piette, "Diary of Fray Juan Crespi," 109.
42. Hewes and Hewes, "Indian Life and Customs," 42.
43. Chávez-García, *Negotiating Conquest*, 6.
44. AOC, "Father Junípero Serra Statue."
45. Phillips, *Vineyards and Vaqueros*, 65.
46. Castillo, *Cross of Thorns*, 119.
47. Beebe and Senkewicz, *Testimonios*, 106–08.
48. McCawley, *First Angelinos*, 194.
49. Rawls, *Indians of California*, 19.
50. McCawley, *First Angelinos*, 191.
51. Similar names were given to the Indigenous groups at other California missions, including Luiseños at Mission San Luis Rey, Fernandeños at Mission San Fernando and Diegueños at Mission San Diego.
52. Rawls, *Indians of California*, 5.
53. Cited in Rawls, *Indians of California*, 35; see also Madley, *American Genocide*, 31.
54. Castillo, *Cross of Thorns*, 141–42.
55. Madley, *American Genocide*, 29–30.
56. Librado, "Breath of the Sun," 23.
57. Castillo, *Cross of Thorns*, 123.
58. Temple, "Toypurina the Witch," 326.

59. Hackel, "Sources of Rebellion," 649.
60. Hackel, "Sources of Rebellion," 655.
61. Hackel, "Sources of Rebellion," 659–60.
62. Other rebellions are described in McCawley, *First Angelinos*, 199.
63. Sandos, "Levantamiento!," 126.
64. Madley, *American Genocide*, 32–34.
65. McCawley, *First Angelinos*, 196.
66. McCawley, *First Angelinos*, 197.
67. Castillo, *Cross of Thorns*, 111.
68. Torres, oral history interview, RLC Archives.
69. Sandos, "Levantamiento!," 118.
70. Rawls, *Indians of California*, 19.

Chapter 2

71. Chávez-García, *Negotiating Conquest*, 18.
72. Rios-Bustamante and Castillo, *Mexican Los Angeles*, 63–64.
73. Rios-Bustamante and Castillo, *Mexican Los Angeles*, 72.
74. Phillips, "Indians in Los Angeles," 399.
75. Mason, "Garrisons of San Diego Presidio," 14–15; Rios-Bustamante and Castillo, *Mexican Los Angeles*, 78.
76. Mason, "Garrisons of San Diego Presidio," 14.
77. Gillingham, *Rancho San Pedro*, 109.
78. Chávez-García, *Negotiating Conquest*, 21.
79. Beebe and Senkewicz, *Testimonios*, 124.
80. Brayer, "Ranchero," 183.
81. Chávez-García, *Negotiating Conquest*, 8.
82. Temple, "Toypurina the Witch," 330.
83. As cited in Gillingham, *Rancho San Pedro*, 92.
84. Engstrand, *Rancho Los Cerritos*, 8.
85. Gumprecht, "51 Miles of Concrete," 435.
86. Fox, *Luis María Peralta*, 13.
87. Baumgartner, *Rancho Santa Margarita*, 29.
88. Black, *Rancho Cucamonga and Doña Merced*, 197.
89. Engstrand, *Rancho Los Cerritos*, 9–10.
90. Faragher, *California: An American History*, 107–08.
91. Beebe and Senkewicz, *Testimonios*, 126.
92. Gillingham, *Rancho San Pedro*, 32.

93. Monroy, "Creation and Re-Creation," 182.
94. Gillingham, *Rancho San Pedro*, 51.
95. Sánchez, *Telling Identities*, 57.
96. Monroy, "Creation and Re-Creation," 179.
97. Hyslop, *Contest for California*, 13.
98. Chávez-García, *Negotiating Conquest*, 68–69.
99. Brayer, "Ranchero," 188.
100. Chávez-García, *Negotiating Conquest*, 68–69.
101. Phillips, "Indians in Los Angeles," 399; Phillips, *Vineyards and Vaqueros*, 303.
102. Chávez-García, *Negotiating Conquest*, 58.

Chapter 3

103. Spitzzeri, *Workman & Temple Families*, 11–12.
104. Spitzzeri, *Workman & Temple Families*, 13.
105. Vásquez, *México*, 39.
106. Spitzzeri, *Workman & Temple Families*, 11.
107. Menke, oral history interview, RLC Archives.
108. Pubols, "California's Mexican Past," 123, 127.
109. Hurtado, *Intimate Frontiers*, 24.
110. Honig, "Presidios of Alta California," 7.
111. Beebe and Senkewicz, *Testimonios*, 215.
112. Beebe and Senkewicz, *Testimonios*, 208–09; Phillips, *Vineyards and Vaqueros*, 62, 75, 78.
113. Hurtado, *Intimate Frontiers*, 31.
114. Beebe and Senkewicz, *Testimonios*, 293.
115. Rios-Bustamante and Castillo, *Mexican Los Angeles*, 113.
116. K. Miller, "Temple Block," 68.
117. Spitzzeri, *Workman & Temple Families*, 20.
118. Spitzzeri, *Workman & Temple Families*, 18.
119. Spitzzeri, *Workman & Temple Families*, 66.
120. From a letter held in the RLC Archives.
121. Phillips, *Vineyards and Vaqueros*, 185.
122. Phillips, "Indians in Los Angeles," 411.
123. Temple, "Dedication of Temple Portraits," 3.
124. Bandini, *Navidad*, 16.
125. Wallace, *Diaries*, August 25, 1856.
126. Chávez-García, *Negotiating Conquest*, 68.

127. Phillips, "Indians in Los Angeles," 404.
128. Oreña, *Reminiscences of Early California*, 37.
129. Black, *Rancho Cucamonga*, 235.
130. Wolman and Smith, *Aloha Rodeo*, 35–38.
131. Black, *Rancho Cucamonga*, 220.
132. Black, *Rancho Cucamonga*, 242.
133. Cited in Phillips, *Vineyards and Vaqueros*, 301.
134. Phillips, *Vineyards and Vaqueros*, 223.
135. Beebe and Senkewicz, *Testimonios*, 43.
136. Phillips, *Vineyards and Vaqueros*, 158.
137. Beebe and Senkewicz, *Testimonios*, 63.
138. S. Smith, *Adobe Days*, 59.
139. Phillips, *Vineyards and Vaqueros*, 301–03.
140. Phillips, *Vineyards and Vaqueros*, 275.
141. Dana, *Two Years Before the Mast*, 131.
142. Roca Barera, *Imperofobia y leyenda negra*, 30, 197–98. See also Rawls, *Indians of California*, 42–43.
143. Beebe and Senkewicz, *Testimonios*, 59.
144. Cherny et al., *Competing Visions*, 4.1.
145. Barrera, *Race and Class*, 13.

Chapter 4

146. Gonzalez, "Making of History," 10.
147. Spitzzeri, *Workman & Temple Families*, 69–71.
148. Faragher, *California: An American History*, 150–58.
149. Spitzzeri, *Workman & Temple Families*, 78–79.
150. Hass, "War in California," 343.
151. Spitzzeri, *Workman & Temple Families*, 79.
152. Beebe and Senkewicz, *Testimonios*, 267–70.
153. Beebe and Senkewicz, *Testimonios*, 20.
154. Gillingham, *Rancho San Pedro*, 151.
155. Temple, letter to Abraham Temple, RLC Archives.
156. Hass, *Conquests and Historical Identities*, 57.
157. Beebe and Senkewicz, *Testimonios*, 295.
158. Madley, *American Genocide*, 70.
159. Cherny et al., *Competing Visions*, 4.2.4.
160. Temple, letter, 1848, RLC Archives.

161. Rohrbough, *Days of Gold*, 66.
162. Rohrbough, *Days of Gold*, 220–24.
163. American Social History Project, https://shec.ashp.cuny.edu. See also Cherny et al., *Competing Visions*, 4.2.7.
164. Cited in Burton, *Men of Achievement*, 65.
165. Rohrbough, *Days of Gold*, 222.
166. Rohrbough, *Days of Gold*, 222.
167. Rohrbough, *Days of Gold*, 90.
168. Cherny et al., *Competing Visions*, 4.3.2.
169. Cherny et al., *Competing Visions*, 4.3.3.
170. Cherny et al., *Competing Visions*, 4.3.2.
171. Hass, *Conquests and Historical Identities*, 58–59.
172. Spitzzeri, *Workman & Temple Families*, 101.
173. Phillips, *Vineyards and Vaqueros*, 162–68.
174. McCawley, *First Angelinos*, 213.
175. Torres, oral history interview, RLC Archives.
176. Cited in Spitzzeri, *Workman & Temple Families*, 91.
177. K. Miller, "Temple Block," 65.
178. Newmark, *Sixty Years*, 287.
179. Newmark, *Sixty Years*, 257.
180. Newmark, *Sixty Years*, 256.
181. Spitzzeri, *Workman & Temple Families*, 95.
182. Gillingham, *Rancho San Pedro*, 141–42.
183. Spitzzeri, *Workman & Temple Families*, 97.
184. Wallace, *Diaries*, August 25, 1856.
185. Keckeisen, "Beyond the Veil," 9.
186. Newmark, *Sixty Years*, 256.
187. Vaughn, "Historical Pageantry," 215, and Rios-Bustamante and Castillo, *Mexican Los Angeles*, 101.

Chapter 5

188. Rohrbough, *Days of Gold*, 1.
189. Rohrbough, *Days of Gold*, 54.
190. Westergaard, "Dr. Thomas Flint," 57.
191. Lorey, *Guide to the Gold Rush*, 80.
192. Smith and Andrews, "Bixby Land Company," 276.
193. Rohrbough, *Days of Gold*, 70.

194. Westergaard, "Dr. Thomas Flint," 59.
195. S. Dudley, *Bixby Family Guide*, 24.
196. Cherny et al., *Competing Visions*, 4.2.5.
197. S. Dudley, *Bixby Family Guide*, 24–26.
198. S. Smith, *Adobe Days*, 24.
199. S. Smith, *Adobe Days*, 45.
200. Rasmussen, "Roots of a Socialite."
201. Katz, *Black West*, 135–36.
202. S. Smith, *Adobe Days*, 21.
203. S. Smith, *Adobe Days*, 125.
204. S. Smith, *Adobe Days,* 52.
205. RLC docent manual.
206. Douglass, "Basque Sheepherding."
207. Saitua, "Basques."
208. S. Smith, *Adobe Days,* 85.
209. Hass, "War in California," 134.
210. California Agricultural Labor Relations Act, signed into law on June 4, 1975.
211. Newton, "William Godfrey," 1.
212. Carter and Bustamante, oral history interview, RLC Archives.
213. S. Smith, *Adobe Days*, 75.
214. S. Smith, *Adobe Days*, 75.
215. Zorbas, *Banished and Embraced*, 15–18.
216. Lew-Williams, *Chinese Must Go*, 22.
217. Chang, *Ghosts of Gold Mountain*, 70.
218. Lew-Williams, *Chinese Must Go*, 32.
219. Lew-Williams, *Chinese Must Go*, 42.
220. Iverson, "Gold Mountain Ranchos."
221. Cherny et al., *Competing Visions*, 6.2.
222. Cherny et al., *Competing Visions*, 6.1.2.
223. Bakken, "Land Policy," 250.
224. S. Dudley, *Bixby Family Guide*, 39.

Chapter 6

225. Engstrand, *Rancho Los Cerritos*, 29.
226. Engstrand, *Rancho Los Cerritos* 27.
227. The Flint, Bixby & Co. partnership that made the original purchase was dissolved after Lewellyn Bixby's death in 1896, resulting in the discontinuance

of the J. Bixby & Co. partnership. A new partnership, the Palos Verdes Co., was incorporated to hold various properties, including Rancho Palos Verdes.

228. "Port of Long Beach History Timeline," https://polb.com/port-info/timeline; Gumprecht, "51 Miles of Concrete"; Gumprecht, *Los Angeles River.*
229. Gumprecht, "51 Miles of Concrete," 470.
230. S. Dudley, *Bixby Family Guide.*
231. Centennial Committee, *Tower of Faith*, 39.
232. "Rapid Population Growth," Calisphere.
233. Burnett, "Japanese Settle."
234. Rimer, "California's Alien Land Laws."
235. S. Smith, *Adobe Days*, 76.
236. Oreña, *Reminiscences of Early California*, 49.
237. Rios-Bustamante and Castillo, *Mexican Los Angeles*, 110–12.

Chapter 7

238. Federal Writers Project, *California in the 1930s*, 202.
239. Faragher, *California: An American History*, 332.
240. Stephen Dudley, oral history interview, RLC Archives.
241. Stephen Dudley, oral history interview, RLC Archives.
242. Engstrand, *Rancho Los Cerritos*, 35.
243. Llewellyn Bixby Sr., oral history interview, RLC Archives.
244. Engstrand, *Rancho Los Cerritos*, 35.
245. "Mission Revival Style 1890s–1920s," NPS.
246. Vaughn, "Historical Pageantry," 215.
247. Long Beach HHS, "Timeline of Racial Inequities."
248. Balderrama and Rodríguez, *Decade of Betrayal*, 68.
249. Faragher, *California: An American History*, 336.
250. Balderrama and Rodríguez, *Decade of Betrayal*, 289–90.
251. Archbold, "Long Beach Is Telling."
252. Archbold, "Long Beach Is Telling."
253. Faragher, *California: An American History*, 347.
254. "Long Beach," California Japantowns.
255. "About Us," Long Beach Day Nursery.
256. Anaya-Morga, "Show de los Caballos."
257. Castillo, *Cross of Thorns,* 208.
258. Wachtel, "Ancient Canoe Revival."
259. "Returning the People's Land," First Nations.

BIBLIOGRAPHY

Anaya-Morga, Laura. "In a Long Beach Parking Lot, Charros Put On 'El Show de los Caballos.'" *Los Angeles Times*, January 25, 2025.

Anderson, M. Kat. *Tending the Wild: Native American Knowledge and the Management of California's Natural Resources.* University of California Press, 2005.

Archbold, Rich. "Long Beach Is Telling Its World War II Story." *Press-Telegram* (Long Beach, CA), September 1, 2017.

Architect of the Capitol (AOC). "Father Junipero Serra Statue." https://www.aoc.gov.

Bakken, Gordon. "Mexican and American Land Policy: A Conflict of Cultures." *Southern California Quarterly* 75, no. 3–4 (1993): 237–62.

Balderrama, Francisco E., and Raymond Rodriguez. *Decade of Betrayal: Mexican Repatriation in the 1930s.* University of New Mexico Press, 2006.

Bandini, Arturo. *Navidad: A Christmas Day with the early Californians.* California Historical Society, 1958.

Barrera, Mario. *Race and Class in the Southwest.* Notre Dame University Press, 1979.

Baumgartner, Jerome. *Rancho Santa Margarita Remembered.* Fithian Press, 1989.

Beebe, Rose M., and Robert M. Senkewicz (eds). *Lands of Promise and Despair: Chronicles of Early California 1535–1846.* University of Oklahoma Press, 2015.

Beebe, Rose M., and Robert M. Senkewicz (eds). *Testimonios: Early California Through the Eyes of Women, 1815–1848.* Heyday Books, 2006.

Black, Esther Boulton. *Rancho Cucamonga and Doña Merced.* San Bernardino County Museum Association, 1975.

Brayer, Herbert O. "Ranchero." *Pacific Historical Review* 12, no. 2 (1943): 181–95.

Burnett, Claudine. "Japanese Settle on Signal Hill." Signal Historical Society. https://www.shhs90755.org/stories-of-the-hill/author-claudine-burnett/cucumber-hill.

Burton, George Ward. *Men of Achievement in the Great Southwest*. Los Angeles Times, 1904.

California Japantowns. "Long Beach." https://www.californiajapantowns.org/longbeach.html.

Calisphere. "1866–1920: Rapid Population Growth, Large-Scale Agriculture, and Integration into the United States." University of California, 2011. https://calisphere.org.

Castillo, Edward. "The Native Response to the Colonization of Alta California." In *Native American Perspectives on the Hispanic Colonization of Alta California*, edited by Edward Castillo. Garland Publishing, 1992.

Castillo, Elias. *A Cross of Thorns*. Craven Street Books, 2015.

Castillo, Pedro, and Antonio Ríos-Bustamante. *México en Los Ángeles, una historia social y cultural, 1781–1985*. Alianza Editorial Mexicana, 1989.

Centennial Committee. *A Tower of Faith in the Heart of the City 1888–1988: Centennial History of the First Congregational Church of Long Beach, California*. Hope Publishing House, 1988.

Chang, Gordon. *Ghosts of Gold Mountain*. Houghton Mifflin Harcourt, 2019.

Chávez-García, Miroslava. *Negotiating Conquest: Gender and Power in California, 1770s to 1880s*. University of Arizona Press, 2004.

Cherny, Robert, Gretchen Lemke-Santangelo, and Richard Griswold del Castillo. *Competing Visions: A History of California*. Published by author, 2005. https://human.libretexts.org/@go/page/132053.

Costrilos, Teresa. "The Dark Side of America's Sheep Industry." *High Country News*, October 2, 2023. https://www.hcn.org.

Crespi, Juan, and Charles Maximin Piette. "An Unpublished Diary of Fray Juan Crespi O.F.M. (San Diego to Monterey, April 17 to November 11, 1770)." *Americas* 3, no. 1 (1946): 102–14.

Dana, Richard Henry. *Two Years Before the Mast*. Waking Lion, 2006.

De Leon, Arnoldo. *Racial Frontiers: Africans, Chinese, and Mexicans in Western America, 1848–1890*. University of New Mexico Press, 2002.

Douglass, William. "Basque Sheepherding in the American West." https://zimmer.fresnostate.edu/~johnca/humanities/Sheep.htm.

Dudley, Stephen. *The Bixby Family Guide*. Bixby Land Company, 2016.

Engstrand, Iris. *Rancho Los Cerritos: A Southern California Legacy Preserved*. Rancho Los Cerritos Foundation, 2009.

Faragher, John Mack. *California: An American History*. Yale University Press, 2022.

Federal Writers Project of the Works Progress Administration. *California in the 1930s: The WPA Guide to the Golden State.* University of California Press, 2013 (originally published 1939).

First Nations. "Returning the People's Land to the Tongva Community." https://www.firstnations.org/stories/returning-the-peoples-land-to-the-tongva-community.

Fisher, Damany. *Discovering Early California Afro-Latino Presence.* Heyday, 2010.

Fox, Frances. *Luis María Peralta and his Adobe.* Smith-McKay Printing, 1975.

Gillingham, Robert. *The Rancho San Pedro.* Rev. ed. Cole-Holmquist Press, Museum Reproductions, 1983 (first edition 1961).

Gonzalez, Michael. "War and the Making of History: The Case of Mexican California, 1821–1846." *California History* 86, no. 2 (2009): 5–68.

Greene, Sean, and Thomas Curwen. "Mapping the Tongva Villages of L.A.'s Past." *Los Angeles Times*, May 9, 2019.

Guinn, J.M. *A History of California and an Extended History of its Southern Coast Counties.* Vol. 2. Historic Record Company, 1907.

Gumprecht, Blake. "51 Miles of Concrete: The Exploitation and Transformation of the Los Angeles River." *Southern California Quarterly* 79, no. 4 (1997): 431–86.

Gumprecht, Blake. *The Los Angeles River.* Johns Hopkins University Press, 1999.

Hackel, Steven. "Sources of Rebellion: Indian Testimony and the Mission San Gabriel Uprising of 1785." *Ethnohistory* 50, no. 4 (2003): 643–69.

Hardwick, Michael. *La Purísima Concepción: The Enduring History of a California Mission.* The History Press, 2015.

Hass, Lisbeth. *Conquests and Historical Identities in California, 1769–1936.* University of California Press, 1995.

Hass, Lisbeth. "War in California, 1846–1848." *California History* 76, no. 2–3 (1997): 331–55.

Heizer, R.F., and M.A. Whipple, eds. *The California Indians: A Source Book.* 2nd ed. University of California Press, 1971.

Heizer, Robert F., and Alan J. Almquist. *The Other Californians: Prejudice and Discrimination Under Spain, Mexico, and the United States to 1920.* University of California Press, 1971.

Hewes, Minna, and Gordon W. Hewes, eds. and trans. "Indian Life and Customs at Mission San Luis Rey: A Record of California Mission Life Written by Pablo Tac, an Indian Neophyte (Rome, ca. 1835)." In *Native American Perspectives on the Hispanic Colonization of Alta California*, edited by Edward Castillo. Garland Publishing, 1992.

Hillburg, Bill. "Pioneer Laments What Happened to Land of His Roots." *Long Beach Press Telegram*, April 1993.

Honig, Sasha. "The Presidios of Alta California." California State Military Museum, 1997. https://www.militarymuseum.org/Presidios.html.

Hurtado, Albert. *Intimate Frontiers: Sex, Gender, and Culture in Old California.* University of New Mexico Press, 1999.

Hyslop, Stephen. *Contest for California: from Spanish Colonization to American Conquest.* Arthur H. Clark Company, 2012.

Iverson, Steven. "Gold Mountain Ranchos: Chinese Workers at Los Alamitos and Los Cerritos, 1872–1890." Presentation at RLC Virtual Volunteer Gathering, June 16, 2020.

Katz, William L. *The Black West.* Rev. ed. Fulcrum Publishing, 2019.

Keckeisen, Katie. "Beyond the Veil: Spiritualism in the Nineteenth Century." Online exhibition of the City of Austin, October 2018. https://www.austintexas.gov/sites/default/files/files/Parks/OHenry/spiritualism.pdf.

Koerper, Henry, Karl Reitz, Sherri Gust, and Steven Iverson. "A Pattern Recognition Study of Cogged Stone Ritual Behavior." *Proceedings of the Society for California Archaeology* 29 (2006): 120–27.

Lake, Alison. *Colonial Rosary: The Spanish and Indian Missions of California.* Swallow Press, Ohio University Press, 2006.

Lew-Williams, Beth. *The Chinese Must Go: Violence, Exclusion, and the Making of the Alien in America.* Harvard University Press, 2018.

Librado, Fernando. "Selections from Breath of the Sun: Life in Early California." In *Native American Perspectives on the Hispanic Colonization of Alta California*, edited by Edward Castillo. Garland Publishing, 1992.

Long Beach Day Nursery. "About Us." https://www.lbdn.org/about-us.

Long Beach Health & Human Services. "Timeline of Racial Inequities in Long Beach." https://www.longbeach.gov.

Lorey, Frank, III. *A Guide to the Gold Rush Country of California.* Arcadia Publishing, 2017.

Lothrop, Gloria Ricci. "Rancheras and the Land: Women and Property Rights in Hispanic California." *Southern California Quarterly* 76, no. 1 (1994): 59–84.

Madley, Benjamin. *An American Genocide: The United States and the California Indian Catastrophe.* Yale University Press, 2016.

Mason, Bill. "The Garrisons of San Diego Presidio, 1770–1794." *Journal of San Diego History*, 24, no. 4 (1978): 1–27.

McCawley, William. *The First Angelinos: The Gabrielino Indians of Los Angeles.* Malki Museum Press, Morongo Indian Reservation, 1996.

Miller, Bruce. *The Gabrielino.* Sand River Press, 1991.

Miller, Kate. "The Temple Block: A Core Sample of Los Angeles History." *Journal of the West* (1994): 62–73.

Monroy, Douglas. "The Creation and Re-Creation of Californio Society." *California History* 76, no. 2–3 (1997): 173–95.

Monroy, Douglas. *Rebirth: Mexican Los Angeles from the Great Migration to the Great Depression.* University of California Press, 1999.

National Park Service. "Mission Revival Style 1890s–1920s." https://www.nps.gov.

Newmark, Harris. *Sixty Years in Southern California, 1853–1913.* Kniekerbocker Press, 1926.

Newton, Frank, Jr. "William Godfrey: Early California Photographer, 1825–1900." *Los Angeles Corral* 188 (1992): 1–8.

Oreña, Dario. *Reminiscences of Early California.* Muleshoe Press, 2011 (originally written 1932).

Phillips, George. "Indians in Los Angeles, 1781–1875: Economic Integration, Social Disintegration." *Pacific Historical Review* (by the Pacific Coast Branch of the American Historical Association) (1980): 395–419.

Phillips, George. *Vineyards and Vaqueros: Indian Labor and the Economic Expansion of Southern California, 1771–1877.* University of Oklahoma Press, 2010.

Pubols, Louise. "Changing Interpretations of California's Mexican Past." *California History* 91, no. 1 (2014): 16–22.

Ramirez, Rose, and Deborah Small. "Saging the World." In *Know We Are Here: Voices of Native California Resistance*, edited by Terra Smith. Heyday Books, 2023.

Rasmussen, Cecilia. "From Roots of a Socialite, a Social Activist Grew." *Los Angeles Times*, January 19, 2003.

Rawls, James. *Indians of California: The Changing Image.* University of Oklahoma Press, 1984.

Reid, Hugo. *The Indians of Los Angeles County: Hugo Reid's Letters of 1852.* Edited and annotated by Robert F. Heizer. Southwest Museum, 1968.

Rimer, Sara. "California's Alien Land Laws." Equal Justice Initiative. https://eji.org/news/californias-alien-land-laws.

Rios-Bustamante, Antonio José, and Pedro G. Castillo. *An Illustrated History of Mexican Los Angeles, 1781–1985.* Regents of the University of California, Chicano Studies Research Center Publications, 1986.

Roca Barera, María Elvira. *Imperofobia y leyenda negra: Roma, Rusia, Estados Unidos y el imperio español.* Ediciones Siruela, 2016.

Rohrbough, Malcom. *Days of Gold: The California Gold Rush and the American Nation.* University of California Press, 1997.

Ruíz, Vicki, and Virginia Sánchez Korrol, eds. *Latina Legacies: Identity, Biography, and Community.* Oxford University Press, 2005.

Ruíz de Burton, María Amparo. *Conflicts of Interest: The Letters of María Amparo Ruíz de Burton.* Arte Publico Press, University of Houston, 2001.

Saitua, Iker. "How Basques Became Synonymous with Sheepherders in the American West." Zócalo Public Square, July 10, 2019. https://www.zocalopublicsquare.org.

Sánchez, Rosaura. *Telling Identities: The Californio Testimonios*. University of Minnesota Press, 1995.

Sandos, James. "Levantamiento!: The 1824 Chumash Uprising Reconsidered." *Southern California Quarterly* 67, no. 2 (1985): 109–33.

Sarris, Greg. "Fidel's Place." In *Know We Are Here: Voices of Native California Resistance*, edited by Terra Smith. Heyday Books, 2023.

Servin, Manuel. "California's Hispanic Heritage: A View into the Spanish Myth." *Journal of San Diego History* 19, no. 1: (1973).

Silliman, Stephen. *Lost Laborers in Colonial California.* University of Arizona Press, 2004.

Smith, A. Maxson, and Thomas F. Andrews. "The Bixby Land Company: A Continuing Family Endeavor." *Southern California Quarterly* 69, no. 3 (1987): 275–85.

Smith, Sarah Bixby. *Adobe Days.* University of Nebraska Press, 1987 (reprint of 3rd ed., 1931).

Smith, Terra, ed. *Know We Are Here: Voices of Native California Resistance.* Heyday Books, 2023.

Spitzzeri, Paul R. *The Workman & Temple Families of Southern California, 1830–1930.* Seligson Publishing, 2007.

Temple, Thomas Workman, II. "Dedication of Temple Portraits." Text of presentation at Rancho Los Cerritos, November 2, 1969, unpublished.

Temple, Thomas Workman, II. "Toypurina the Witch and the Indian Uprising at San Gabriel." *Masterkey* 32, no. 5 (1958): 136–52.

Vásquez, Josefina Zoraida. *México al tiempo de su guerra con Estados Unidos (1846–1848).* El Colegio de México, Secretaría de Relaciones Exteriores, Fondo de Cultura Económico, 1997.

Vaughn, Chelsea. "The Joining of Historical Pageantry and the Spanish Fantasy Past: The Meeting of Señora Josefa Yorba and Lucretia del Valle." *Journal of San Diego History* 57, no. 4 (2011): 213–36.

Wachtel, Ileana. "Ancient Canoe Revival Highlights Indigenous Sustainability Practices and Ocean Conservation." USC Dornsife, College of Letters, Arts and Sciences, April 4, 2024. https://dornsife.usc.edu.

Wallace, William. *William Allen Wallace Diaries, 1854 August 25–1858 April 1.* Beineke Library, Yale University.

Westergaard, Waldemar. "Diary of Dr. Thomas Flint: California to Maine and Return, 1851–1855." *Annual Publication of the Historical Society of Southern California* 12, no. 3 (1923): 53–127.

Wolman, David and Julian Smith. *Aloha Rodeo.* HarperCollins, 2019.

Zorbas, Elaine. *Banished and Embraced: The Chinese in Fiddletown and the Mother Lode.* Mythos Press, 2015.

Unpublished Interviews (In Rancho Los Cerritos Archives)

Arias, Aurelio. Oral history interview by Fredrica Whyte. Main Library, Long Beach, CA. November 12, 1966.

Babcock, Virginia Coronado. Oral history interview by Roberta Nichols. Rancho Los Cerritos, July 16, 1972.

Berner, Loretta. Oral history interview by Fredrica Whyte. Rancho Los Cerritos, March 26, 1966.

Bixby, Llewellyn, Jr. Oral history interview by Ann Andriesse. Rancho Los Cerritos, January 1984.

Bixby, Richard. Oral history interview. Rancho Los Cerritos, June 15, 1962.

Bushong, Katherine. Oral history interview by Loretta Berner. Rancho Los Cerritos, September 12, 1967.

Carter, Clarinda Bustamante, and Salvador Bustamante. Oral history interview by Loretta Berner and Fredrica Whyte. Rancho Los Cerritos, April 26, 1966.

Coronado, Frank. Oral history interview by Fredrica Whyte and Roberta Nichols. Virginia Country Club, Long Beach, CA, 1968.

Davies, Arthur. Oral history interview by Fredrica Whyte. North Branch Library, Long Beach, CA, April 7, 1965.

De Cigaran, Alphonso. Oral history interview by Michelle Lord. Rancho Los Cerritos, July 11, 1992.

Dudley, Paul, Jr. Oral history interview by Steve Iverson. Rancho Los Cerritos, February 11, 2000.

Dudley, Stephen. Oral history interview by Tory Inloes. Rancho Los Cerritos, May 13, 2014.

Encinas, Alfred. Oral history interview by Roberta Nichols. Rancho Los Cerritos, September 17, 1968.

Houghton, Mark. Oral history interview by Roberta Nichols. Main Library, Long Beach, CA, November 25, 1971.

Liera, Manuel, and Concepción Coronado Liera. Oral history interview by Roberta Mickey Mellevold and Ellen Calomiris. Rancho Los Cerritos, September 16, 1989.

Liera, Manuel, and Concepción Coronado Liera. Oral history interview by Roberta Nichols. Rancho Los Cerritos, November 1, 1970.

Liera, Manuel, and Concepción Coronado Liera. Oral history interview by Mickey Mellevold and Cilla Temple. Rancho Los Cerritos, September 12, 1992.

Menke, Nellie King. Oral history interview by Loretta Berner and Fredericka Whyte. Included as part of oral history interview with Dorothy Andrews Ortley. Rancho Los Cerritos, March 26, 1966.

Smith, Jean Bixby, and Barbara Bixby Blackwell. Oral history interview by Steve Iverson. Rancho Los Cerritos, February 28, 2002.

Sugiyama, Kimi. Interview summary. Rancho Los Cerritos, February 6, 1980.

Torres, Craig. Oral history interview by Sarah FitzGerald and Andreyina Juarez. Rancho Los Cerritos, June 4, 2018.

Valenzuela, Alfred. Oral history interview by Roberta Nichols. Rancho Los Cerritos, March 30, 1968.

ABOUT THE AUTHOR

Dr. Leslie Reese holds a BA in anthropology from Stanford University; an interdisciplinary MA from California State University, Long Beach (CSULB) in linguistics, Mexican American studies and education; and a PhD from UCLA in comparative education. Currently a professor emerita from CSULB, she has collaborated with colleagues in Spain, Mexico and the United States on research projects, including studies of linguistic minority rights, culturally responsive education and home-school connections with immigrant students and families.

Leslie remembers visiting Rancho Los Cerritos as a fourth-grade student, a visit that fostered a lifelong interest in California history and in the Rancho in particular. She and her husband, Ron, have been volunteer docents at the Rancho since 1992 and were among the founders of the Hispanic History

Committee. Leslie has done archival research to support RLC exhibitions and has made presentations on the life of Rafaela Cota de Temple and on the Tenant Era of RLC history. Her daughter, Alana, carries on the family tradition, currently working as education coordinator at Rancho Los Cerritos. In her spare time, Leslie enjoys travel, playing the ukulele and working with Living Waters for the World on the installation of water purification projects in Peru.

Visit us at
www.historypress.com